JOSEPH RABIE

CBT
FOR MANAGING
STRESS AND
ANXIETY

12-WEEK COGNITIVE BEHAVIORAL THERAPY PROGRAM

Table of Contents

Introduction :

Lheart that breaks, thoughts that swirl, a lump in the stomach... Stress and anxiety invade our lives insidiously, nibbling away at our joy and energy. They deprive us of our sleep, sabotage our relationships and prevent us from living fully. Anxiety is a normal response of the body to a perceived stress or threat. It manifests as feelings of fear, worry, and apprehension. While anxiety can be beneficial in some situations, as we will see later, it can become problematic when it is excessive or out of control.

During my career, I have met hundreds of patients struggling with anxiety in all its forms: panic attacks, phobias, obsessive-compulsive disorder, generalized or work-related anxiety or social relationships... These people were going through hell on a daily basis. Some had given up their studies, their work; others felt trapped in routines that prevented them from leading a normal life or forming fulfilling relationships. I still remember Lou, paralyzed at the idea of leaving her house because she was convinced that an imminent danger was waiting for her; Marc who had his hands bleeding to the point of recurring fear of germs; or Claire who, eaten away by permanent doubt, checked 50 times if she had turned off the gas before leaving her apartment... I also witnessed their immense relief, even rebirth, when they freed themselves from these impediments thanks to a targeted therapy: the so-called cognitive-behavioral therapy.

You probably bought this book because you suffer from anxiety or related disorders yourself – or someone close to you suffers this ordeal on a daily basis. Whatever form this pervasive anxiety takes (phobias, compulsions, panic attacks...), I want to tell you first: you are not alone. In France, between 8 and 12% of the population is affected by these ailments to varying degrees. All over the world, anxiety and depression are the main reasons for consultation in psychiatry. During my career, I have received in my practice hundreds of people of all ages and backgrounds who thought they had no choice but to undergo. But what these people do not know is that there are effective solutions to free themselves from these mental disorders. Yes, it is possible to truly and sustainably heal your anxieties thanks to a proven method: cognitive behavioral therapy.

Scientifically validated for nearly 40 years, based on recent advances in neuroscience, CBT is now recommended by the who as a first-line treatment for anxiety disorders. Its results are as conclusive as some drugs, especially in the long term, with remission rates exceeding 70% according to studies. Through the pages of this book, discover how CBT can defuse irrational fears, short-circuit the brain mechanisms that cause anxiety, and profoundly modify your automatic reactions to stress. Through practical exercises and step-by-step monitoring, you will gradually regain control of your thoughts, emotions and existence.

Duration: 12 weeks

In the last part of the book you will find your 12-week program that will literally transform your relationship with anxiety and stress. Whatever the form or forms your disorders take (generalized anxiety, phobias, OCD, panic disorders, etc.), this cognitive and behavioral program has been proven to achieve significant remission or even complete recovery in more than 70% of patients according to studies.

Why 12 weeks? Because this is the recommended standard time to observe profound and lasting changes in the psychological mechanisms that sustain your anxiety. We will literally reprogram your dysfunctional thought patterns, automatic stress responses, and avoidance strategies.

Yes, it is possible to turn your back on a lifetime of anxiety and experience a new freedom! This guide will get you there. So take heart and embark now on the path of your healing!

Part 1: Understanding Anxiety and Stress

Chapter 1: Definitions and Mechanisms.

Let's dive into the deep waters of anxiety and stress, exploring the subtle nuances that set them apart. Let's uncover the mysteries of the physical and psychological manifestations that accompany them, and dive into the meanders of the brain to understand the complex mechanisms that underlie these states of mind. Prepare for a captivating adventure, where knowledge blends with discovery to illuminate our path to a deeper understanding of ourselves.

Anxiety / Stress

Over the course of evolution, stress has played a crucial role in man's survival, enabling him to react quickly to the dangers and threats of his environment. When our ancestors lived in caves, stress was a valuable ally that helped them stay alert and respond effectively to predators and potential dangers. This stress-triggered "fight or flight" response was essential to ensure their survival and safety.

Example: Imagine a group of prehistoric men hunting in the savannah. Suddenly, a lion appears from the bushes, threatening the safety of the group. Faced with this imminent threat, the bodies of prehistoric men react instantly to stress. Their pupils dilate to improve vision, their heart beats faster to deliver more oxygen to the muscles, and their digestive system slows down to save energy. These physiological reactions allow men to remain alert and react quickly to ensure their survival. Stress plays a crucial role in helping us stay alert and make quick decisions to avoid danger. Without this stress response, they may be unable to respond effectively to danger, putting our lives at risk.

Transition to anxiety: However, in the modern world, stress can become problematic when it turns into chronic anxiety. While acute and short-term stress can be beneficial, chronic and persistent stress can have detrimental effects on mental and physical health. When stress becomes chronic, it can lead to prolonged activation of the stress response system, which can lead to anxiety disorders.

Why does chronic stress become anxiety? Chronic stress can turn into anxiety due to several factors. First, prolonged exposure to stress can lead to desensitization of cortisol receptors, the stress hormone, which can lead to dysregulation of the stress response. In addition, imbalances in neurotransmitters, such as serotonin and GABA, may also contribute to the development of anxiety.

The difference between anxiety and stress

The difference between anxiety and stress lies mainly in their nature and origin.

Stress: Stress is a normal reaction of the body to a situation perceived as a threat or pressure. This can be a response to external events such as deadlines at work, family issues, or personal challenges. Stress is usually short-lived and goes away once the stressful situation is resolved.

Example of stress
➢ **Situation:** You are late for an important appointment. ➢ **Thoughts:** "I'm going to be late." "I will lose my job." I will lose my job ➢ **Emotions:** Agitation, nervousness, impatience. ➢ **Physical manifestations:** Increased heart rate, sweating, muscle tension.

Anxiety: Anxiety, on the other hand, is a more intense and prolonged reaction. It is characterized by persistent apprehension, a sense of worry and nervousness, often with no obvious cause. Anxiety may be more generalized and not related to a specific situation. It may also be accompanied by physical symptoms such as headaches, fatigue, sleep disturbances and muscle tension.

Example of anxiety:
➢ **Situation:** You need to take an important exam next week. ➢ **Thoughts:** "I'm going to fail." "I suck at …" "I'm going to be disappointed in myself." ➢ **Emotions:** Worry, fear, nervousness, restlessness. ➢ **Physical manifestations:** Sleep disturbances, headaches, fatigue, difficulty concentrating.

The Main Difference: The main difference between stress and anxiety lies in their origin and duration. Stress is usually a response to an external, short-term situation, while anxiety is more internal, often with no identifiable cause, and may be more persistent.

> ➤ Anxiety is often related to anticipated events, while stress is usually caused by present situations.
> ➤ Anxiety can be chronic, while stress is usually acute.
> ➤ Anxiety can manifest as more intense and varied symptoms than stress.

Similarities

> ➤ Anxiety and stress can both negatively impact physical and psychological well-being.
> ➤ Both can be treated with relaxation and stress management techniques.
> ➤ In some cases, anxiety and stress may require drug therapy or treatment.

Understanding the differences between anxiety and stress is key to identifying the source of your difficulties and choosing the most appropriate treatment.

It should be remembered that stress and anxiety are normal human experiences and that everyone can experience them at some point in their lives. However, if stress or anxiety becomes overwhelming or interferes with daily life, it is recommended to consult a mental health professional for appropriate help and advice.

Physical and psychological manifestations:

Anxiety and stress can manifest themselves in different ways, both physically and psychologically.

1. Stress:

> **Muscle tension:** Stress can lead to muscle tension, especially in the neck, shoulders and back.
> **Headaches:** Tension headaches are common when under stress, and can be felt as a squeeze or pressure around the head.
> **Digestive problems:** Stress can disrupt the normal functioning of the digestive system, leading to stomach upset, bloating, or diarrhea.
> **Fatigue:** Chronic stress can lead to persistent fatigue, even after adequate rest.

2. Anxiety

> **Heart palpitations:** Anxiety can cause a faster heartbeat, palpitations, or strong heartbeat sensations.
> **Shortness of breath:** People with anxiety may experience a feeling of shortness of breath or difficulty breathing, even in the absence of physical activity.
> **Sweating:** Anxiety can cause excessive sweating, especially in the palms, armpits and forehead.
> **Trembling:** Some anxious people may experience uncontrollable trembling, especially in the hands.

Psychological Manifestations of Stress and Anxiety:

1. Stress:

> **Irritability:** Stress can make a person more irritable, which can affect their relationships with others.
> **Difficulty concentrating:** Stress can lead to decreased concentration and the ability to focus on tasks.

> **Feeling overloaded:** Stressed people may feel overwhelmed by their responsibilities and struggle to manage their workload.
> **Insomnia:** Stress can disrupt sleep, leading to difficulty falling asleep, frequent awakenings, or non-restorative sleep.

2. Anxiety

> **Excessive worry:** Anxiety is characterized by excessive and persistent worry about future situations, even if they are unlikely.
> **Fear and panic:** Anxious people may experience irrational fears or sudden panic attacks, often accompanied by intense physical symptoms.
> **Feelings of imminent danger:** Anxiety can give the impression that imminent danger or impending disaster is imminent, even in the absence of a real threat.
> **Avoidance:** To cope with their anxiety, some people may avoid situations or places that trigger their anxiety, which can lead to a deterioration in quality of life.

Conclusion: Physical and psychological manifestations of stress and anxiety can vary from person to person and can be influenced by various factors such as personality, past experiences and environmental factors. Recognizing these manifestations is essential for identifying and effectively managing stress and anxiety.

BRAIN MECHANISMS

The brain mechanisms involved in stress and anxiety are complex and involve several brain regions as well as specific neurotransmitters. Here is a simplified overview of these mechanisms with a concrete example of a daily life situation:

Situation: Marie is about to go through a job interview for a highly coveted position. She feels nervous and anxious about this important meeting.

BRAIN MECHANISMS

1. The amygdala:

- *Function:* The amygdala is a key brain region involved in processing emotions, especially fear and anxiety.
- *Involvement:* In Marie's case, her amygdala becomes overactive in response to the stress of the interview. This can trigger a fear or anxiety response, contributing to his feelings of nervousness.

2. Hypothalamus:

- *Function:* The hypothalamus regulates emotions and stress responses.
- *Involvement:* The amygdala sends signals to Mary's hypothalamus, thereby triggering the release of stress hormones, such as cortisol, into her bloodstream, reinforcing her state of anxiety.

3. Prefrontal cortex

- *Function:* The prefrontal cortex regulates emotions and behaviors.
- *Involvement:* In a stressful situation like Marie's, her prefrontal cortex may be less active, which can impair her ability to regulate her emotions and make rational decisions about the interview.

4. Neurotransmitters:

- *Noradrenaline and serotonin:* Involved in mood and stress regulation, imbalances in these neurotransmitters may contribute to Marie's anxiety.
- *GABA:* As an inhibitory neurotransmitter, a low level of GABA may also be associated with Marie's feelings of anxiety.

Analyse :

In this example, the brain mechanisms related to Mary's anxiety are clearly observable. Her amygdala reacts to the stress of the interview by becoming overactive, triggering a cascade of neurochemical and neural reactions that reinforce her state of anxiety. The prefrontal cortex, which normally regulates emotions, may be less effective in these situations, contributing to Mary's inability to calm her worries. Imbalances in neurotransmitters, such as norepinephrine, serotonin, and GABA, may also play a role in intensifying her anxiety.

Conclusion: This example illustrates how brain mechanisms, such as amygdala activation, hypothalamus response, prefrontal cortex functioning, and neurotransmitter imbalances, interact to produce an anxiety response in Marie when faced with a stressful situation. This understanding can be useful in developing stress and anxiety management strategies.

The role of sympathetic and parasympathetic system

They are two branches of the autonomic nervous system, which regulates involuntary body functions such as breathing, heart rate, digestion, and stress response. These two systems work in tandem to maintain homeostasis, the internal balance of the body, but they often have opposite effects.

1. Sympathetic System: The sympathetic system is often associated with the body's "fight or flight" response to stress. When a threat is perceived, whether real or perceived, the sympathetic system is activated. This triggers a series of physiological responses, such as increased heart rate, pupil dilation, release of adrenaline and norepinephrine, and redirection of blood flow to skeletal muscles. These responses prepare the body to respond quickly to the perceived threat, either by fighting the threat or by running away.

2. Parasympathetic System: In contrast, the parasympathetic system is often referred to as the "rest and digestion response." It is activated when the body is in a state of calm and rest, promoting recovery, digestion and relaxation. The effects of the parasympathetic system include decreased heart rate, constriction of the pupils, stimulation of digestion and relaxation of the muscles. When the parasympathetic system is active, it promotes relaxation and recovery, helping the body return to a state of balance after a period of stress or intense activity.

Stress, fear and anxiety

- In situations of prolonged or chronic stress, the sympathetic system may be over-activated, which can lead to anxiety symptoms, such as increased muscle tension, rapid and shallow breathing, and increased blood pressure.

- Chronic activation of the sympathetic system can also contribute to long-term health problems, such as hypertension, cardiovascular disease, and anxiety disorders.

- The balance between the sympathetic and parasympathetic system is crucial for maintaining an adaptive stress response and promoting overall well-being.

In summary, the sympathetic system and the parasympathetic system play essential roles in the response to stress and anxiety. Appropriate activation of these systems is necessary to respond effectively to stressful situations and promote recovery and relaxation when stress decreases.

Chaptre 2 : Causes and risk factors

Dive into the depths of anxiety with us, exploring the many facets that make up anxiety. In this captivating chapter, we'll look at the causes and risk factors that shape this complex human experience. Explore with us the influences of the environment, genetics, life experiences and personal beliefs that come into play in the formation of anxiety. Get ready for a deep dive, where the mysteries of anxiety will be unraveled in a new light.

Environmental Factors

The environment in which we live and evolve plays a crucial role in our mental well-being. Environmental factors can be a major source of stress and anxiety, which can contribute to some people's predisposition to developing these disorders. Imagine a butterfly with fragile wings, tossed about by the merciless winds of a storm. This is the feeling of helplessness that often grips the victims of stress and anxiety, prisoners of an invisible web woven by the forces of the environment. Far from being passive bystanders, our environment exerts an insidious influence on our mental well-being, shaping our reactions to stress and anxiety. Far from being inevitable, understanding these harmful influences offers us the keys to regaining control of our emotional destiny.

Take the case of Sarah, a bright and ambitious young woman, caught up in the hellish whirlwind of an all-consuming professional life. Harassed by ruthless deadlines, drowned in an avalanche of endless tasks, Sarah finds herself overwhelmed by a sense of helplessness and exhaustion. Sarah's professional environment, far from being a simple neutral setting, turns out to be a real stress nest. Excessive workload, lack of control over his assignments, deleterious work climate, all these factors contribute to fueling his growing anxiety.

This is only one example. The environment, whether professional, family, social or economic, can turn into an inexhaustible source of stress and anxiety. Social pressure, family conflicts, financial precariousness, environmental insecurity, all these elements constitute invisible dangers that threaten our emotional balance.

Stress and anxiety: adaptive responses. Environmental stress can take many forms, such as work pressures, family conflicts, financial difficulties, or traumatic events. Faced with these challenges, our body reacts by releasing stress hormones, thus preparing our body to react. However, when stress becomes chronic or excessive, it can have detrimental effects on our mental health, which can contribute to the development of anxiety.

Individual Predisposition and Sensitivity to Stress: Each individual reacts differently to environmental stress based on a variety of factors, including their genetic predisposition, personal history, and coping mechanisms. Some people may be more sensitive to stress than others, which can make them more vulnerable to the development of anxiety. It is therefore essential to recognize and respect these individual differences in managing environmental stress.

Genetic factors:

If the environment acts like a sculptor, shaping our sensitivity to stress and anxiety, our genes are the raw material on which it works. Imagine two trees, one sturdy and the other frail, exposed to the same storm. The sturdy tree, thanks to its deep roots and strong wood, will bend but not break. The frail tree, on the other hand, will be more likely to break under the force of the wind. Similarly, our genes can predispose us to react differently to stress and anxiety.

Some people are born with increased sensitivity, inheriting a genetic variation that makes them more likely to experience stress and anxiety. Others, on the other hand, appear to have natural genetic armor that protects them from these disorders.

Let's take the example of two twin sisters, Clara and Lila. Raised in the same family and social environment, they seem to experience stress and anxiety in diametrically opposite ways. Clara is easily overwhelmed by stressful situations, while Lila seems to handle them with disconcerting ease. Scientific studies have revealed that genes may play an important role in this difference in sensitivity. Certain genetic variations have been associated with greater susceptibility to stress and anxiety. **For example,** a particular gene, known as 5-HTTLPR, influences how the body responds to serotonin, a neurotransmitter that plays a crucial role in regulating mood.

How do I know if I am predisposed to stress and anxiety?

Apart from consulting a geneticist, there are other ways to determine if you are genetically predisposed to stress and anxiety, or if you have genetic variations such as the 5-HTTLPR gene. Here are some options:

1) **Online genetic testing:** There are online genetic tests that claim to be able to identify genetic variations associated with stress and anxiety. However, it is important to note that these tests may not be as accurate or reliable as tests performed by healthcare professionals.
2) **Family history:** If you have a family history of anxiety disorders or stress, this may indicate a genetic predisposition. Talking with your loved ones about their own mental health experiences can give you clues about your own risk.
3) Mental **Health Professional Assessment: A mental health** professional, such as a psychiatrist or psychologist, can assess your medical history, symptoms, and family history to determine if you have a genetic predisposition to stress and anxiety.
4) **Symptom self-assessment:** If you frequently experience symptoms of stress and anxiety, this may also indicate a genetic predisposition. Keep a diary of your symptoms and their frequency to discuss with a healthcare professional.

But it must be understood that genes are not necessarily a life sentence. Even if you are genetically predisposed to stress and anxiety, it does not mean that you are doomed to suffer from these disorders. Many environmental and behavioral factors can influence how your genes express themselves. For example, by taking positive steps to take care of your mental well-being, you can mitigate the impact of your genetic predispositions and lead a more fulfilling and less stressful life.

Life Experience

Life experiences play a crucial role in how we respond to stress and anxiety. Our past experiences, social interactions, successes and failures shape our perception of the world and influence our mental health. Here's how life experiences can contribute to predisposition to stress and anxiety:

1) **Trauma and stressful events:** Traumatic events, such as abuse, serious accidents, or the loss of a loved one, can have a profound impact on our mental health. These experiences can trigger acute stress responses and, if left untreated, can contribute to the development of anxiety disorders. For example, Marie witnessed a serious car accident as a child. This traumatic experience triggered panic attacks and an intense fear of driving or even getting into a car, which had a significant impact on her quality of life and made her more vulnerable to stress and anxiety.

2) **Chronic stress:** Situations of prolonged stress, such as financial problems, family conflicts or work pressures, can also play a role in predisposing to stress and anxiety. Chronic stress can disrupt the brain's hormonal and neurochemical balance, increasing the risk of anxiety disorders. For example, Sarah grew up in a family where emotions were rarely expressed or discussed. As a result, she struggles to recognize and manage her own emotions, making her more likely to experience stress and anxiety in situations where she feels overwhelmed.

3) **Models of behaviour learned:** Life experiences can also influence how we learn to manage stress. If we grew up in an environment where stress was poorly managed or ignored, we may struggle to develop healthy stress management strategies, which can make us more vulnerable to anxiety.

4) **Social support:** Social support, or lack thereof, may also play a role in predisposing to stress and anxiety. Healthy relationships and emotional support can help alleviate the effects of stress, while social isolation can worsen anxiety symptoms. For example, David lost his spouse a few years ago and since then he has struggled to find emotional support. The lack of close relationships and social support left him feeling isolated and alone, which contributed to his anxiety and sense of emotional distress.

In conclusion, life experiences play an important role in predisposing to stress and anxiety. By understanding how our past experiences can influence our mental health, we can take steps to improve our emotional well-being and reduce our vulnerability to anxiety disorders.

Beliefs and Thoughts:

Our thoughts and beliefs are not mere abstractions, they are a powerful force that can influence our perception of the world and our reaction to stress and anxiety. Imagine two people who are in the same stressful situation, for example, an important exam. One, convinced of her abilities and confident in her success, will approach the exam with serenity. The other, inhabited by negative thoughts and doubts about their skills, will be much more likely to experience stress and anxiety. This inner dialogue, often unconscious, can play a crucial role in amplifying or decreasing stress and anxiety.

Some beliefs and thoughts promote stress and anxiety:

- **Catastrophism:** Systematically anticipate the worst possible scenario.
- **Binary thinking:** See everything in black or white, no shades.
- **Negative Focus:** Focus only on the negative aspects of a situation.
- **Excessive self-criticism:** Constantly denigrating and criticizing oneself.
- **Perfectionism:** Demanding unattainable perfection from oneself.

Conversely, other thoughts and beliefs can help reduce them:

- **Positive thinking:** Focusing on the positive aspects of a situation.
- **Rationalization:** Analyze the situation objectively and realistically.
- **Relativization:** Decrease the importance of stressful events.
- **Self-confidence:** Trusting yourself and believing in your abilities.
- **Acceptance:** Accepting situations you can't control.

Learning to identify and change the thoughts and beliefs that fuel stress and anxiety is a powerful tool for improving your mental well-being.

I propose you to place

- Become aware of your inner dialogue.
- Identify negative thoughts and beliefs.
- Challenge these thoughts and replace them with more positive alternatives.
- Develop more rational and realistic thinking.
- Cultivate self-confidence and acceptance.

By mastering your inner dialogue, you can regain control of your emotional life and build a more serene and fulfilled existence. Never forget, your thoughts and beliefs are not reality. You have the power to transform them and create a more positive and calming inner reality.

How do mental filters work?

We all have filters in our heads through which all information from outside passes. Becoming aware of the existence of these filters is the first step in working on your approach. And changing your approach is the most effective way to positively revolutionize your personal development.

For starters, I have a challenge for you:

Below you will see a video in which two teams pass the basketball in both directions. Your task is to count the number of passes the white shirt team will make. It sounds easy, but it turns out that only 10% of people are able to correctly calculate the number of passes! Let's see if you're in that group. Remember: focus on the number of passes between players on the white team.

PLEASE: stop playback and watch the video

Title of the video: concentration! How many ball passes the team makes.
Video link: https://youtu.be/mO3m1HCzakY

Simply scan this QR code with your phone to access the video

In case the video has been deleted, please search YouTube for one of these requests:

- CONCENTRATION How many ball passes does the team "in white" make?

- Selective attention test
- The Monkey Business Illusion

Very important: Please play along. Continue reading once you have completed the task.

So, what about that? You probably think the task was very simple. I have bad news for you. The number of apps doesn't really matter here. The question is whether you saw a man dressed as a gorilla walking between the players passing the ball to them. If not, watch the movie again, this time without worrying about the number of passes.

What's amazing is that the vast majority of people don't see this gorilla. Focusing on a particular task limits them to seeing only a fragment of reality. When looking for a specific piece of information, it will be very difficult for you to notice anything else, even if it is something as strange and absurd as a walking gorilla! This is how the filters of our mind work. Like a sieve, they only let through specific and selected information.

How Does it Work?

The first filters are **your senses.** They already eliminate some of the information about reality. When you look at the world around you, you are limited by the structure of your brain. As you've probably noticed, you don't see everything with the naked eye - you don't notice the force of gravity, the sound waves, the infrared light. So it turns out that you don't see reality as it really is. What you see is your brain's interpretation of it. In fact, your way of seeing the world can be very far from the truth. Maybe the brains of other animal species see a "more real" reality? Perhaps a dog's brain is closer to perceiving the true nature of the world, even if it perceives it in a completely different way than humans? We have absolutely no evidence that it is our species that sees the world as it really is.

Other filters are already acquired during life. **These are the experiences** that create your personality from birth. These are the values that have been instilled in you for many years by parents, school and society. These are your ambitions and expectations. And most importantly, your beliefs about the world. Beliefs that create the way you perceive the whole world, your own life, your abilities, and your relationships with others. If you believe that the world is a vile and devious place, you will act as if it is. This will make you have many unpleasant emotions and experiences. But if you believe that the world is a wonderful and beautiful place, your life will be completely different.

Each belief leads to certain behaviours.

Suppose for a moment that you believe that everyone is lying and wants to take advantage of you. Now imagine how you would behave with new people if you had this conviction. Now suppose you are convinced that people like to meet new people and that everyone has something special in them. How are you now? You can only change your sensory filters by taking certain drugs. By intoxicating your brain, you make it perceive reality differently. While drinking a few beers, you may have noticed that the world is completely different then:).

The most important thing, however, is that you can successfully modify the operation of this second group of filters. You can change your relationship with your past experience. You can change your expectations for the future. You can change your beliefs about the world around you. These changes lead to the most important and profound changes in your emotions, habits and behaviours. So start looking deeper. Instead of changing your individual behaviors, change your beliefs. A different way of looking at the world is a completely different life. Remember that you always have "mental glasses" on your eyes. These glasses can be black, and they can be a source of misery, because you will see everything around you in black and it causes you great stress for the slightest problem or obstacle of everyday life. They can also be colored, which will make the world an interesting, peaceful and wonderful place for you.

The purpose of this chapter is to remind you and encourage you to take action. Your approach is important for your development, if you don't know it yet, start changing your approach and the whole world will change and of course you will have a life with zero stress. It all starts in your head, so to change your attitude and stop being stressed, you have to turn to the thoughts you feed on, and succeed in destroying your negative thought habits.

Let's go back to our video: Admit it, have you noticed a gorilla?:)

Cognitive distortions.

Mental filters, also known as cognitive distortions, are automatic and distorted thought patterns that influence how we perceive events, situations, and interactions with others. These distortions can contribute to stress and anxiety by distorting our perception of reality and generating negative and irrational thoughts. Here are some examples of common mental filters and their impact on stress and anxiety:

The Disaster Filter: This filter is about expecting the worst in all situations, even in the absence of hard evidence. For example, a person using this filter might think that losing their job will lead to a series of financial and personal disasters, even if they have never faced them before.

Dichotomous thinking (all or nothing): This distortion involves seeing things in absolute terms, without nuances or compromises. For example, a person might think that they are a total failure if they do not achieve perfection in all areas of their life, which can lead to considerable stress and anxiety.

Excessive generalization: This filter consists of drawing general conclusions from a single negative event or experience. For example, if a person fails an exam, they might generalize thinking they are stupid or incapable in all areas of their life.

The Emotional Thinking Filter: This distortion involves assuming that our emotions reflect reality. For example, if a person feels anxious in a social situation, they may conclude that they are actually in danger, even if this is not the case objectively.

The "guessing" mentality: This filter consists of interpreting the actions and intentions of others in a negative way, without sufficient evidence to support it. For example, a person might think that their friends no longer like them simply because they didn't invite them on a date, when there might be other valid explanations.

These mental filters can help increase stress and anxiety by amplifying negative thoughts and feeding destructive thought patterns. Awareness of these cognitive distortions is an important first step in overcoming them and adopting more realistic and balanced thoughts. Cognitive behavioral therapy (CBT) is often used to help individuals identify and modify these mental filters in order to reduce their stress and anxiety.

Junk Food and Brain: A Time Bomb for Mental Health.

Who has never succumbed to the temptation of a fat burger or a pizza dripping with cheese? Junk food, with its intense flavors and promise of instant gratification, is a real trap for our taste buds and our brain. But behind this fleeting pleasure lies a much less glowing _reality: junk food can have a deleterious impact on our mental health, especially by increasing our vulnerability to stress, anxiety, and depression_. Junk food, such as fast foods like McDonald's, Burger King and sugar-rich soft drinks, can have detrimental effects on our mental health by disrupting the reward system in the brain. These foods are often high in simple sugars, saturated fats and empty calories, which can lead to dysfunction of the reward system and increase the risk of stress, anxiety and depression.

Under the microscope

To understand how junk food affects our mental health, we first need to look at how the reward system in our brain works. This system is governed by a neurotransmitter, dopamine, which is released in response to pleasurable stimuli, such as food. When we consume junk food, which is high in sugar and fat, our brains are flooded with dopamine, which creates a feeling of intense pleasure. **It's a bit like taking a dose of drugs:** the brain gets used to this high level of dopamine and asks for it again, creating an addiction to junk food.

The flipside?

The problem with junk food is that this pleasure is fleeting. _**The dopamine spike is followed by a fall, which can leave us in a state of fatigue, irritability and low morale.**_ In addition, regular consumption of junk food can upset the balance of other neurotransmitters involved in mood regulation, such as serotonin and norepinephrine.

A vicious loop

Excessive consumption of junk food can lead to a dysfunction of the reward system. By dint of consuming foods high in sugars and fats, our brains can become less sensitive to dopamine, which means we need more food to feel the same level of pleasure.

In addition, stress, anxiety, and depression can also prompt us to turn to junk food for comfort. **It's a vicious cycle:** junk food worsens the symptoms of these disorders, prompting us to consume even more. This can lead to overeating and contribute to the development of obesity.

An impact on long-term mental health.

Scientific studies have shown that regular consumption of junk food can increase the risk of developing mood disorders, such as depression. **Indeed, junk food can disrupt the functioning of the hippocampus, a region of the brain involved in the regulation of emotions.**

Solutions to get out of the trap

The good news is that it is possible to get out of the trap of junk food and its harmful effects on mental health. A few tips:

- **Keep to a healthy diet**
- **Limit sugar and fat intake.**
- **Manage stress through relaxation techniques.**
- **A mental health practitioner will be available for support, if necessary.**

Final Thoughts

Junk food is not just about taste pleasure. **It can have a real impact on our mental health, increasing our vulnerability to stress, anxiety and depression.** By taking care of our diet and living a healthy lifestyle, we can preserve our mental health and overall well-being.

Let's not forget that our brain is a precious organ that must be protected. Junk food can be a poison to our mental health. **Let's choose to feed it healthy and nourishing food to allow it to run at full speed.**

Chapter 3: Assessing Your Anxiety and Stress.

Understanding stress and anxiety is an essential first step, but to get to know yourself better and identify the sources of your discomfort, a thorough assessment is necessary. This chapter offers you a series of tools and questionnaires to help you assess your anxiety and stress levels objectively and reliably.

Inventories and self-assessment scales.

Inventories and self-assessment scales are valuable tools for assessing your level of anxiety and stress. They are designed to help you identify and quantify your symptoms, which can be useful for tracking your progress over time and determining the effectiveness of the interventions you put in place. Here are some of the most commonly used inventories and scales in this context:

1. Hamilton Anxiety Scale (HAM-A):

This scale is often used by healthcare professionals to assess the severity of anxiety. It includes 14 items that assess symptoms such as tension, nervousness, and fears. For each item, indicate the degree to which you have experienced each symptom over the past week using the following scale:

0 = No symptoms | 1 = Mild | 2 = Moderate | 3 = Severe | 4 = Very severe

Inventory: Hamilton Anxiety Scale (HAM-A).

1) Feelings of fear	9. Feeling tired
2) Voltage	10. Difficulty concentrating
3) Insomnia	11. I feel a lump in my throat.
4) Difficulty relaxing	12. Short breath sensations
5) Nervosity	13. Heartbeat palpitations
6) EXCITABILITY	14. Excessive sweating (clammy hands.
7) Irritability	
8) Feeling weak	

For each symptom, check the box that best matches your experience over the past week. Once you're done, calculate your total score by adding the answers for each item. Your total score may give you an indication of how severe your anxiety is, but it's always best to see a healthcare professional for a full assessment.

Score explanation:

- ➢ **A total score of 0 to 7** is considered normal and indicates minimal anxiety.
- ➢ **A total score of 8 to 14** suggests mild anxiety.
- ➢ **A total score of 15 to 23** indicates moderate anxiety.
- ➢ **A total score of 24 to 30** indicates severe anxiety.
- ➢ **A total score of more than 30** indicates very severe anxiety.

It is important to note that this test is not a substitute for a professional assessment and it is best to consult a healthcare professional for an appropriate assessment.

2. Beck's Anxiety Scale (BAI):

This scale is designed to measure the severity of anxiety in adults and adolescents. It includes 21 items assessing symptoms such as fear, nervousness and difficulty relaxing.

Instructions: For each statement below, please indicate to what extent it applies to you at this time, using the following scale:

0 = Not at all | 1 = Slightly | 2= Moderately | 3 = Severely

Beck Anxiety Inventory (BAI)

1. Feelings of fear, dread or panic:
2. Feelings of dizziness, weakness or empty head:
3. Heartbeat or palpitations:
4. Tremor (e.g. hand tremor):
5. Excessive sweating (for no apparent reason):
6. Feelings of breathlessness or choking:
7. Chest pain or discomfort:
8. Abdominal nausea or discomfort:
9. Feeling of a lump in the throat or difficulty swallowing:
10. Feelings of heat or chills:
11. Numbness or tingling:

12. Chills or hot flushes
13. Fear of losing control or going crazy
14. Fear of dying
15. Feeling of detachment from oneself or reality (depersonalization)
16. Fear of doing something shameful or ridiculous:
17. Feelings of not being in control of one's actions, or of doing things without thinking about them (depersonalization):
18. Fear of being in crowded places, traveling alone, or leaving home alone:
19. Feelings of nervousness, restlessness or feeling of being on the verge of a nervous breakdown:
20. Weak, restless feelings in the legs.
21. Feelings of muscle tension or stiffness:

Result:

To get your total score, add up the scores for each item. Your total score can range from 0 to 63. Here's how to interpret your score:

- ➢ **0-7:** No anxiety
- ➢ **8-15:** Mild anxiety
- ➢ **16-25:** Moderate anxiety
- ➢ **26-63:** Severe anxiety

Please note that this questionnaire is a self-assessment tool and does not replace a professional diagnosis. If you have any concerns about your anxiety level, please consult a qualified mental health professional.

3. State-Trait Anxiety Inventory (STAI):

This inventory measures both state anxiety (the anxiety felt at a given time) and trait anxiety (a person's general level of anxiety). It is often used in research studies to assess anxiety.

Instructions for the State-Trait Anxiety Inventory (STAI)

For each question, rate the extent to which you experienced the condition described <u>over the past week</u> using the 1 to 4 scale. Answer questions based on your usual feelings, without focusing on specific events that may have temporarily affected your morale. However, if these events have had a significant impact on your anxiety over the past week, it's only natural that this will be reflected in your responses. The objective is to provide a general assessment of your anxiety level, taking into account normal fluctuations related to everyday life events.

1. **Not at all:** You have not felt this state at all.
2. **A little:** You have felt this state to some extent.
3. **Enough:** You have felt this state to a great extent.
4. **Very:** You have felt this state to a very great extent.

Answer honestly and as accurately as possible. There are no right or wrong answers. They include

1. - I'm feeling calm,
2. I feel tense.
3. I feel comfortable.
4. I feel nervous and agitated.
5. I feel at peace
6. I feel relaxed.
7. I feel more confident
8. I feel ina hurry.
9. I feel satisfied with myself.
10. I feel upset.
11. I feel safe.
12. I feel restless.
13. I feel confused.
14. I feel anxious
15. I feel happy.
16. I feel kind of unsettled!"
17. I'm in a good mood.
18. I'm concerned.
19. - I'm feeling calm,
20. I feel good about myself.
21. **Result:**

Add your scores for questions 2, 4, 8, 10, 12, 14, 18, and 20 to get your state anxiety score. Add your scores for questions 1, 3, 5, 6, 7, 9, 11, 13, 15, 16, 17, and 19 to get your trait anxiety score. Compare your scores with the following ranges to interpret your anxiety levels:

State Anxiety Score:	**Trait Anxiety Score:**
➢ 20-40: Low anxiety	➢ 20-34: Low anxiety
➢ 41-60: Moderate anxiety	➢ 35-49: Moderate anxiety
➢ 61-80: High anxiety	➢ 50-64: High anxiety
➢ 81-100: Very high anxiety	➢ 65-80: Very high anxiety

4. Perceived stress scale (PSS) :

The Perceived Stress Scale (PSS) is designed to measure a person's overall perception of the amount of stress they feel in their life. It consists of 10 questions, which you need to answer based on your feelings and experiences over the past few weeks.

Instructions: For each question, please indicate how much you agree with the statement using a scale from 0 to 4, where 0 means "never" and 4 means "very often". Answer honestly based on how you currently feel.

➢ **0 =** Never
➢ **1 =** Rarely
➢ **2 =** Occasionally
➢ **3 =** Often ·
➢ **4 =** Very often

Perceived Stress Inventory (PSS):

1. In the last few weeks, how unpredictable have you found the situations in your life to be?
2. In the last few weeks, to what extent have you found things out of your control?
3. In the last few weeks, how unpredictable did you find your life?
4. In the last few weeks, how well did you find things going the way you wanted them to?
5. In the last few weeks, to what extent have you found it difficult to control the irritations in your life?

6. In the last few weeks, to what extent have you found things going from bad to worse for you?

7. In the last few weeks, to what extent have you found that you were able to cope with all the problems that life brought you?

8. In the last few weeks, to what extent have you found that things are not going as you expected?

9. In the last few weeks, to what extent did you find that you were in control of your life?

10. In the last few weeks, to what extent did you find that you could easily solve the problems that presented themselves?

Add up the scores for each question to get a total score. A higher score indicates a higher level of perceived stress.

➢ **0 to 13: Low perceived stress**. You have a relatively low perception of stress in your daily life.

➢ **14-26: Perceived moderate stress**. You experience an average level of stress in your life, which can impact your emotional well-being.

➢ **27-40: Perceived high stress**. You have a high perception of stress in your life, which can have a significant impact on your mental and physical health.

Échelle visuelle analogique (VAS) :

This scale consists of a 10 cm horizontal line, with ends marked **"not at all"** and **"extremely"**. People mark a dot on the line to indicate their level of anxiety or stress.

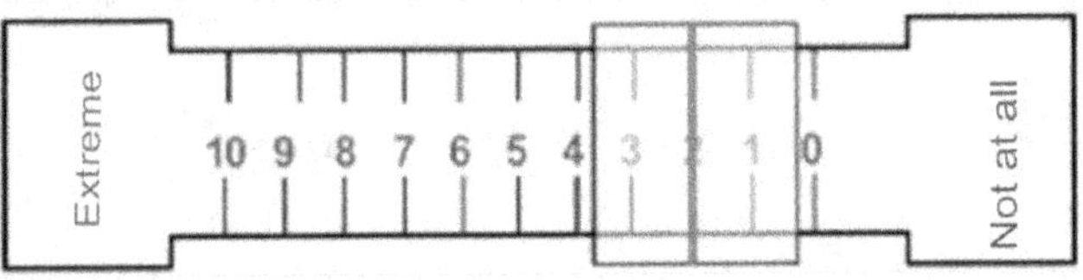

Here are instructions for using the Visual Analog Scale (VAS) to assess your level of anxiety and stress:

1. **Preparation:** Find a quiet place where you can focus without being interrupted. Have a pencil and a ruler or other method for measuring centimeters.

2. **Positioning:** Draw a 10 cm horizontal line on a sheet of paper. Mark the ends of the line as "not at all" on the far left and "extremely" on the far right.

3. **Assessment:** Reflect on your current level of anxiety or stress. Based on this scale, where would you place a point on the line to indicate your current level? For example, if you are very anxious or stressed, you could place your point near the "extremely" end. If you feel calm and relaxed, you could place your point near the "not at all" end.

4. **Measure:** Use the ruler to measure the distance in centimeters between the point you placed and the "not at all" end. This will give you a number that represents your level of anxiety or stress on the 0-10 scale.

5. **Interpretation:** The higher the number, the higher your level of anxiety or stress. For example, a number close to 0 indicates a low level of anxiety or stress, while a number close to 10 indicates a high level. When interpreting your results, consider how you feel overall and how often you experience these emotions.

This scale can help you better understand your own level of anxiety and stress, which can be helpful in tracking your progress over time and identifying situations that may be causing you the most stress. If you find that your anxiety or stress levels are high and interfering with your daily life, it may be helpful to consult a mental health professional for additional support.

These tools can be used independently or in conjunction with a mental health professional to assess your anxiety and stress. They can provide valuable information to help you better understand your emotions and develop an appropriate management plan.

Therapeutic writing: How to keep a diary?

Keeping a logbook is a great way to self-assess your own level of anxiety and stress. You can use a notebook, diary, or even a dedicated mobile app. Take time each day to sit quietly, focus on your emotions, and write them down honestly and sincerely. Feel free to use keywords or short sentences if you are short on time, the important thing is to record your feelings regularly and conscientiously. By keeping a logbook, you can develop a better understanding of your emotions and thoughts, which can help you manage your anxiety and stress more effectively.

This is how you can proceed:

- **Objective:** Over a period of one week, you will keep a logbook to record your emotions and thoughts in order to better understand the situations that trigger your anxiety and stress.
- **Frequency of writing:** You commit to writing in your journal once a day, preferably at the end of the day to reflect on the events of the day.
- **Write about your emotions:** Every day, take a few minutes to sit in a quiet place and reflect on your day. Write down the emotions you felt, such as anxiety, stress, fear, anger, sadness, or any other significant emotions. Also describe how you felt physically, such as muscle tension, headaches, palpitations, etc.
- **Identify patterns:** As you reread your diary at the end of the week, try to spot common patterns or triggers of your anxiety and stress. For example, you might notice that difficult social interactions often trigger your anxiety, or that tight deadlines at work stress you out.
- **Take regular assessments:** At the end of the week, take stock of your writings to assess your level of anxiety and stress over the days. Write down the days when you felt particularly anxious or stressed, as well as the days when you felt calmer and more relaxed. This can help you identify the factors that contribute most to your anxiety and stress, as well as strategies that have been effective in helping you manage them.

By keeping a logbook, you can develop a better understanding of your emotions and thoughts, which can help you manage your anxiety and stress more effectively.

Identify their thought patterns.

Thought patterns are automatic, unconscious patterns that influence how we perceive the world, interpret ourselves, and interact with others. They can be positive or negative, and they usually form from our lived experiences, especially during childhood. Identifying one's thought patterns is essential to understanding how our thoughts influence our emotions and behaviors. These thought patterns are like filters through which we perceive the world, and they can have a significant impact on our emotional well-being.

The Origin of Negative Thoughts:

It is quite normal to have negative thoughts from time to time. However, if you constantly feel them, it may indicate an underlying problem. Here are some possible reasons why you always have negative thoughts:

1) **Automatic thoughts:** These are thoughts that arise spontaneously in your mind without you having solicited them. They can be negative, positive or neutral. In your case, it seems that you have a lot of negative automatic thoughts.

2) **Cognitive distortions:** These are thinking mistakes that can make your negative thoughts more intense and unrealistic. There are several types of cognitive distortions, including:
   - **Catastrophism:** You imagine that the worst will always happen.
   - **Mental filters:** You only focus on the negative aspects of a situation and ignore the positive ones.
   - **Mind Reading:** You think you know what others think of you, without any evidence.
   - **Labelling:** You define yourself by your mistakes or failures.

3) **Low self-esteem:** If you have low self-esteem, you tend to devalue yourself and think that you are not able to succeed. This can lead you to have negative thoughts about yourself, your abilities, and your chances of success.

4) **Stress and anxiety:** Stress and anxiety can also contribute to negative thoughts. When you are stressed or anxious, your brain is alert and is more likely to generate negative thoughts.

5) **Trauma and negative experiences:** If you have experienced trauma or negative experiences in the past, it can also make you more likely to have negative thoughts.

6) **Depression: Depression** is a mental illness that can cause symptoms such as negative thoughts, sadness, loss of interest in activities, and sleep disorders.

What if you still have negative thoughts?

You need to identify your thought patterns can help you become aware of negative thoughts that contribute to your anxiety and stress. By recognizing them, you can begin to replace them with more positive thoughts. Here's how:

1. **Observation:** Take a moment to observe your thoughts in different situations. Write down thoughts that come to mind when you are faced with challenges or stressful situations. For *example*: Imagine that you have an important project to complete. Your thoughts might be, "I'm going to fail," "I'm not good enough," or "Everything's going to go wrong."

2. **Identification:** Once you have observed your thoughts, try to identify recurring patterns. These patterns can be negative thoughts, catastrophic thoughts, or perfectionist thoughts, among others. For *example*: You realize that in many stressful situations, you tend to think catastrophically, imagining the worst possible scenario.

3. **Assessment:** Evaluate your thought patterns to determine if they are realistic and helpful. Ask yourself if these thoughts are based on hard facts or unfounded assumptions, and if they help you solve problems or make you more anxious. For *example*: You realize that your catastrophic thoughts are not based on real facts, but rather on irrational assumptions.

4. **Replacement:** Finally, try to replace your negative thought patterns with more positive and realistic thoughts. This can help you reduce your anxiety and stress. For *example*: Instead of thinking "I'm going to fail," you might think "I'm going to do my best and learn from this experience, regardless of the outcome."

But it's childish that, my state will not change by changing sentences in my head? It is understandable to feel skeptical about the impact of changing your thoughts on your emotional state. However, there is strong evidence supporting the effectiveness of this approach. Consider the following:

1. **Brain plasticity:** Studies have shown that our brains are able to restructure in response to new experiences, including new ways of thinking. By consciously changing our thoughts, we can strengthen positive neural connections that contribute to increased emotional well-being.

2. **Cognitive Behavioral Therapies (CBTs):** CBTs, which focus on changing negative thought patterns, are widely recognized as effective in treating anxiety, depression, and other mental health issues. These therapies are

based on the principle that changing our thoughts can lead to a change in our emotions and behaviors.

3. **Effect of thoughts on emotions:** Our thoughts have a direct impact on our emotions. For example, if we constantly think negatively, we are more likely to feel anxious, sad, or angry. By changing our thoughts to more positive and realistic thoughts, we can positively influence our emotional state.

4. **Impact on emotions:** Studies have shown that our thoughts can alter our brain chemistry and affect our emotional state. For example, negative thoughts can increase the production of cortisol, the stress hormone, while positive thoughts can stimulate the production of endorphins, the "happiness hormones."

5. **Effect on well-being:** Research in positive psychology has shown that replacing negative thoughts with positive ones can improve emotional well-being and reduce symptoms of depression and anxiety.

6. **Influence on behaviour:** Our thought patterns also influence our behaviours. For example, if you tend to think catastrophically, you can avoid situations that challenge you, limiting your opportunities for personal growth.

7. **Holistic approach:** Changing one's thoughts is only part of a holistic approach to mental health. Combined with other strategies such as practicing relaxation techniques, physical exercise, and social support, changing thought patterns can help significantly improve your emotional well-being.

In summary, while it may seem simple, changing your thoughts can have a significant impact on your emotional state and quality of life. This can take time and practice, but many people have seen noticeable improvements by taking a proactive approach to changing their thought patterns.

Part 2: CBT to Treat Anxiety and Stress

Chapter 1: CBT Principles and History.

CBT was developed in the 1960s by psychiatrists Aaron Beck and Albert Ellis. They observed that patients with depression often had negative and irrational thoughts that contributed to their condition. So they developed techniques to help patients identify and change these negative thought patterns, which gave rise to CBT.

Cognitive and Behavioral Therapy (CBT) is a therapeutic approach widely used to treat a variety of emotional and psychological problems. It is based on the premise that our thoughts, emotions, and behaviors are intertwined, and that by changing our thoughts and behaviors, we can influence our emotions and overall well-being.

Imagine your brain as a garden:

- ➢ **Thoughts:** These are the seeds you plant.
- ➢ **Emotions:** These are the flowers that grow from these seeds.
- ➢ **Behaviours:** These are the actions you take to maintain your garden.

The principle of protection against unfair competition was closely connected with intellectual property.

By changing the seeds you plant (your thoughts) and taking care of your garden (your behaviors), you can influence the flowers that grow (your emotions).

For example:

- ➢ **Negative thinking:** "I suck."
- ➢ **Emotion:** Sadness and discouragement.
- ➢ **Behavior:** Stay locked in your home and avoid social interactions.

By changing thinking:

- ➢ **New thinking:** "I have skills and qualities."
- ➢ **Emotion:** Motivation and self-confidence.
- ➢ **Behaviour:** Going out of the house, meeting new people and engaging in positive activities.

Explanation:

- ➢ **CBT = Gardening:** Taking care of your mental garden to cultivate positive emotions.
- ➢ **Thoughts = Seeds:** Choose the seeds (thoughts) that will nourish the flowers (emotions) that you want to see bloom.
- ➢ **Behaviours = Watering and maintenance:** Taking care of your garden (mind) by adopting healthy and positive behaviours.

In short, CBT allows you to take control of your mental garden and cultivate the emotional well-being you deserve.

This therapeutic approach is based on several key concepts:

1. **Thoughts Influence Emotions:** CBT recognizes that our thoughts play a crucial role in how we feel. For example, if we have constant negative thoughts, we are more likely to feel sad, anxious, or angry.
2. **Emotions influence behaviors:** Our emotions also impact our behaviors. For example, if we are anxious, we might avoid situations that make us uncomfortable, which can reinforce our anxiety in the long run.
3. **Behaviors influence thoughts:** Our behaviors can also affect our thoughts. For example, if we act positively and proactively, we are more likely to think positively.

By changing our negative thought patterns and maladaptive behaviors, CBT aims to improve our emotional well-being. This approach relies on techniques such as cognitive restructuring, which involves identifying and replacing negative thoughts with more realistic and positive ones, as well as behavioral techniques such as progressive exposure, which involves gradually confronting feared situations to reduce anxiety.

In summary, CBT is an effective therapeutic approach that helps individuals better understand and modify their thoughts, emotions, and behaviors to improve their emotional well-being and quality of life.

Different generations of cognitive therapies.

Cognitive therapies have evolved over decades, each bringing new ideas and techniques to help people manage their thoughts and emotions more effectively. Here is an overview of the different generations of cognitive therapies:

1. **First generation:** The first generation of cognitive therapies emerged in the 1960s and 1970s, primarily through the work of Aaron Beck and Albert Ellis. These therapies focused on modifying patients' negative and irrational thoughts, using techniques such as cognitive restructuring and Socratic dialogue. For example, a patient with social anxiety identifies negative automatic thoughts ("I'm going to make a fool of myself") and replaces them with more rational thoughts ("I'm able to handle this situation").

2. **Second generation:** In the 1980s and 1990s, a second generation of cognitive therapies emerged, placing more emphasis on patients' underlying thought patterns and core beliefs. These therapies, like Jeffrey Young's Pattern Therapy, aimed to identify and modify deep-rooted thought patterns that contributed to patients' emotional problems. For example, a depressed patient discovers a pattern of abandonment thinking and learns to challenge it and develop healthier beliefs about relationships.

3. **Third generation:** The third generation of cognitive therapies is newer and focuses on concepts such as mindfulness and acceptance. Approaches like Acceptance and Commitment Therapy (ACT) and Mindfulness-Based Cognitive Behavioral Therapy (MBCT) seek to help patients accept their thoughts and emotions without judgment, which can reduce their impact on their emotional well-being. For example, an anxious patient learns to observe their thoughts and emotions compassionately and without judgment, thereby reducing their impact on their well-being.

4. **Integration of approaches:** Nowadays, many practitioners integrate different cognitive approaches according to the individual needs of patients. For example, a therapy may combine elements of traditional

CBT with mindfulness techniques or thought pattern-based approaches. For example, a patient combines classical CBT to identify negative thoughts with mindfulness to manage and accept them with more serenity.

In conclusion, cognitive therapies have come a long way since their inception, and their evolution continues to bring new perspectives and more effective approaches to help people manage their thoughts and emotions.

Why is it effective ?

Cognitive Behavioural Therapy (CBT): Emotional gardening to cultivate well-being. Its effectiveness is based on a solid scientific foundation and a logical approach that resonates both intellectually and emotionally.

Scientific evidence

- **Rigorous studies:** Hundreds of scientific studies have demonstrated the effectiveness of CBT in treating various psychological disorders, such as anxiety, depression, phobias, and obsessive-compulsive disorder.
- **Efficacy comparable to drugs:** CBT is often as effective as drugs for the management of certain disorders, and offers the advantage of being a non-invasive and side-effect-free approach.
- **Adaptable process:** CBT is a flexible therapy that is adaptable to the specific needs of each individual. The therapist can adjust techniques and interventions according to the progress and characteristics of the patient.

Emotional logic:

- **Link between thoughts, emotions, and behaviors:** CBT recognizes the interconnection between our thoughts, emotions, and behaviors. By modifying one of these elements, we can influence the others.
- **Learning new skills:** CBT offers practical tools and techniques that can be applied on a daily basis to identify and change negative thoughts, adopt healthy behaviours and manage difficult emotions.
- **Empowerment and Accountability:** CBT encourages the patient to take an active role in their healing process. He becomes an actor of his change and develops skills to better manage his mental health.

Analogy of Emotional Gardening:

> - **Cultivating wellbeing:** CBT is similar to emotional gardening where the patient learns to cultivate positive thoughts, manage emotions and adopt healthy behaviours to flourish and flourish.
> - **Self-Care:** CBT encourages the patient to take care of their "mental garden" by investing in practices that nurture their emotional well-being.
> - **A continuous process:** The maintenance of a garden is a constant work. Similarly, CBT is part of a process of learning and personal development that continues beyond therapy.

In conclusion, CBT is an effective and scientifically validated approach to cultivating emotional well-being and improving quality of life. Its emotional logic and adaptability make it a valuable tool for anyone who wants to take control of their mental health and flourish towards a more serene and fulfilling future.

Chapter 2: Cognitive Techniques.

In this chapter, we will explore the cognitive techniques that lie at the heart of cognitive behavioral therapy (CBT). These approaches, derived from decades of research and clinical practice, aim to change thought patterns and beliefs that contribute to emotional disorders. We'll look at how cognitive restructuring, decentralization and mindfulness meditation, as well as altering automatic thoughts, can help improve our emotional well-being and quality of life. Through exercises and concrete examples, we will discover how to put these techniques into practice to transform the way we think and live.

Cognitive Restructuring

Cognitive restructuring is a key technique in cognitive behavioral therapy (CBT) that aims to alter negative or irrational thought patterns that contribute to emotional disorders such as depression and anxiety. This approach is based on the principle that our thoughts influence our emotions and behaviors, and that by changing our thoughts, we can change the way we feel and act. Imagine wearing distorting glasses that make you see the world in a negative way. These glasses represent your negative thought patterns. Cognitive restructuring involves removing these distorting glasses and replacing them with glasses that allow you to see the world more realistically and positively. For example, if you tend to think "I'm a failure" when you make a mistake, cognitive restructuring would encourage you to replace that thought with something more realistic and constructive like "I make mistakes sometimes, but that doesn't mean I'm a failure as a person."

The Cognitive Carpentry Workshop: Sculpting Positive Thoughts

Imagine your mind as a carpentry workshop.

> ➢ **Thoughts:** These are the wooden blocks you use to create your sculptures.
> ➢ **Emotions:** These are the sculptures you create from these wooden blocks.
> ➢ **Cognitive restructuring:** This is the art of transforming blocks of raw thoughts into sculptures of hope and well-being.

- ➤ **Negative thoughts:** They can be like deformed and misshapen wooden blocks that create imperfect and fragile carvings.
- ➤ **Cognitive restructuring:** It allows you to work on these wooden blocks, smooth and polish them to create solid and beautiful sculptures.

How does it work?

1. Identify negative thoughts:

- ➤ **Spot automatic thoughts:** Those that arise spontaneously in your mind without you having solicited them.
- ➤ **Analyze your thoughts:** Ask yourself if your thoughts are realistic and evidence-based.
- ➤ **Notice the impact of your thoughts:** How do your thoughts influence your emotions and behaviors?

2. Transforming Negative Thoughts:

- ➤ **Challenge your thoughts:** Challenge the cognitive distortions and thinking mistakes that fuel your negative thoughts.
- ➤ **Develop alternative thoughts:** Look for evidence that supports more positive and realistic thoughts.
- ➤ **Apply specific techniques:** Cognitive restructuring offers several techniques to modify your thoughts, such as **cognitive decentering**, the **ABC method** or the **Socratic questions technique**.

For example:

- ➤ **Negative thinking:** "I will fail my exam."
- ➤ **Cognitive Distortion:** Catastrophism - "I am unable to achieve anything."
- ➤ **Thought challenge:** "Did I really fail all my exams? Are there any situations where I've been successful?"
- ➤ **Alternative Thinking:** "I have skills and have worked hard. If I continue to review and prepare, I have a good chance of succeeding."

> - **Cognitive restructuring = Woodworking workshop:** Turning negative thoughts into positive ones is like turning raw wooden blocks into refined and elegant sculptures.
> - **Negative thoughts = Raw wood blocks:** They can be misshapen and difficult to work with, limiting your creativity and potential.
> - **Positive Thoughts = Refined Sculptures:** They are beautiful, solid and allow you to create a more positive and fulfilling life.

In conclusion, cognitive restructuring is a powerful tool to transform your mental workshop and shape a more positive and fulfilling life. By practicing cognitive restructuring, you can change the way you perceive events in your life and reduce your stress and anxiety levels. This can help you take a more balanced and constructive perspective, which can improve your emotional well-being and quality of life.

Decentration and mindfulness meditation.

Decentering and mindfulness meditation are cognitive behavioral therapy (CBT) techniques that aim to cultivate an attentive and peaceful awareness of one's thoughts, emotions and sensations. These practices can help reduce stress, anxiety, and depression by allowing individuals to step back from their thoughts and emotions and observe them in a detached and objective manner. Imagine that your mind is like a sky filled with clouds. Thoughts and emotions are the passing clouds, but instead of getting carried away by them, decentering and mindfulness meditation help you stay in the sky, watching the clouds pass without clinging to them. Decentering is taking a step back from one's thoughts and emotions, observing them as transient mental events rather than objective realities. This reduces identification with one's thoughts and emotions, which can contribute to greater emotional stability.

Mindfulness meditation, on the other hand, involves paying close attention to the present moment, focusing on one's physical sensations, breathing or thoughts, without judgment. This helps to cultivate a greater awareness of oneself and one's environment, which can reduce stress and anxiety. For example, if you are feeling anxious about a future situation, decentering and mindfulness meditation would allow you to take a step back from that anxiety, observing it as a normal mental reaction rather than an inevitable reality. This can help you manage your anxiety more effectively and reduce its impact on your emotional well-being. Here's how it works

Mindfulness practice

1) **Find a quiet place:** Choose a place where you won't be disturbed and where you feel comfortable.
2) **Adopt a comfortable posture:** Sit or lie down in a comfortable position. Back is straight and relaxed.
3) **Focus on your breathing:** Focus on your breathing. Observe how air enters and leaves your lungs, without trying to control it.
4) **Be aware of your thoughts:** Let your thoughts come and go, without judging them. Gently bring your attention back to your breathing whenever you realize your mind is wandering.
5) **Be aware of your sensations:** Also pay attention to the physical sensations of your body, such as tension, tingling or pain, always remaining in an attitude of benevolence towards yourself.
6) **Practice regularly:** Try practicing mindfulness meditation for a few minutes each day. Gradually increase the length of your sessions as you feel more comfortable.
7) **Integrate mindfulness into your daily life:** like eating, walking or taking a shower, being fully present in every moment.

The Socratic question technique:

The technique of Socratic questions, also called maieutic, is a method of learning and reflection from ancient Greek philosophy. It consists of asking a series of benevolent and open-ended questions to get the interlocutor to explore their own thoughts, clarify their ideas and discover their own truths. Socrates, the originator of this technique, did not claim to hold the truth, but rather to help people give birth to their own wisdom. He used the art of questioning to stimulate critical thinking and challenge preconceived ideas.

Here are some key principles of the Socratic Questioning Technique:

> - **Ask open-ended questions** that cannot be answered with a simple "yes" or "no".
> - **Listen carefully** to the answers of the interlocutor and reformulate his words if necessary.
> - **Do not give direct answers**, but rather encourage the interlocutor to think for themselves.
> - **Use questions to explore the implications** of the interlocutor's ideas and arguments.
> - **Respect the opinions of the interlocutor**, even if they differ from yours.

The Socratic questions technique can be used in many contexts, such as:

> - **Education**: to encourage students to think critically and develop their own understanding of the world.
> - **Coaching**: to help clients identify their goals and find solutions to their problems.
> - **Management**: to promote collaboration and collective decision-making.
> - **Daily life**: to improve communication and mutual understanding.

Here are some example prompts:

> - Can you define for me what you mean by...?
> - What evidence supports your claim?
> - What are the implications of this position?
> - What about other factors?
> - How does this situation make you feel?
> - What would you like to get out of this situation?

The Socratic Questions Technique is a powerful and challenging tool that can help you learn, reflect, and grow. By using it constructively and respectfully, you can improve your communication, critical thinking, and problem-solving skills.

Example of Socratic questions for the case of stress and anxiety:

Situation: You are preparing an important presentation and you feel a strong sense of stress and anxiety.

Socratic Questions

- ➢ What stresses you the most in this situation?
- ➢ What thoughts are running through your mind right now?
- ➢ Are these thoughts based on reality or irrational fears
- ➢ What could go wrong if your presentation went wrong
- ➢ Is it worth worrying so much about a hypothetical event?
- ➢ What are your strengths and skills that can help you succeed in your presentation?
- ➢ What can you do concretely to reduce your stress and anxiety?
- ➢ Have you experienced similar past situations? How did you manage them?
- ➢ Have you learned from your experiences?
- ➢ How can you use these learnings to cope with the current situation?

By answering these questions honestly and thoughtfully, you can:

- ➢ Understand the causes of your stress and anxiety.
- ➢ Identify irrational thoughts that contribute to your discomfort.
- ➢ Develop more rational and positive thoughts.
- ➢ Put in place concrete strategies to manage your stress and anxiety.

It is important to note that the Socratic questions technique is not a silver bullet. It requires time, patience and regular practice. However, it can be a valuable tool to help you better manage your stress and anxiety, and improve your quality of life.

Here are some tips for using the Socratic questions technique effectively:

- ➢ Ask questions in a spirit of openness and kindness.
- ➢ Listen carefully to your interlocutor's answers without judging them.
- ➢ Don't give direct answers, but encourage them to think for themselves.
- ➢ Use a calm, composed tone.
- ➢ Be patient and persistent.

In conclusion, the Socratic questions technique is a simple and powerful method to learn how to manage stress and anxiety. By using it regularly and thoughtfully, you can improve your mental and emotional well-being.

The ABC method in CBT:

The ABC method is a simple and effective technique. It makes it possible to understand and modify the links between our thoughts, emotions and behaviours. The ABC model is based on the idea that our emotions are not directly caused by external events, but rather by our interpretations of those events. These interpretations, or beliefs, may be rational or irrational.

The acronym VoIP stands for

- ➤ **A: Activation** (the outside event)
- ➤ **B: Beliefs** (beliefs and thoughts)
- ➤ **C: Consequences** (emotions and behaviours)

Here's how the ABC method works:

1. **Identify the external event** (A) that triggered a negative emotion.
2. **Write down the thoughts and beliefs** (B) that crossed your mind at that time.
3. **Analyze your thoughts**: are they rational or irrational? Are there any cognitive distortions?
4. **Identify the consequences** (C) of your thoughts: emotions felt and behaviors adopted.
5. **Refute your irrational thoughts** and replace them with more rational and positive thoughts.
6. **Observe changes** in your emotions and behaviors.

The ABC method can be used to manage many difficult situations, such as:Anxiety, anger, depression, stress, negative thoughts, maladaptive behaviors...

Example of ABC Method Application for Stress and Anxiety:

Situation: You are driving on a busy highway and you are starting to feel stress and anxiety.

A - Activation (the external event):

- ➤ You're on a busy highway.
- ➤ There is a lot of traffic and cars are moving fast.
- ➤ You feel in a hurry to reach your destination.

B - Beliefs:

- ➢ "I'm going to have an accident."
- ➢ "I'm going to get lost."
- ➢ "I'm not able to drive in these conditions."
- ➢ I'm going to be late.
- ➢ "Everyone's going to honk my horn."

C - Consequences (emotions and behaviours):

- ➢ You feel an increase in stress and anxiety.
- ➢ Your heart is beating rapidly
- ➢ You have cold sweats.
- ➢ It's hard to concentrate.'
- ➢ You want to get off the highway.

Challenging thoughts:

- ➢ *"Am I really in danger? Are there any statistics that prove I'm more likely to have an accident on a busy highway?"*
- ➢ *"Have I ever had an accident in the past? Am I a safe driver?"*
- ➢ *"Is being late really that important?"*
- ➢ *"What would others think if I told them I was having trouble driving on the highway?"*

Alternative Thoughts:

- ➢ *"I am a capable driver and I can handle this situation."*
- ➢ *"I'll take my time and drive carefully."*
- ➢ *"If I feel too stressed, I can stop at a rest area."*
- ➢ *"It's normal to feel stress from time to time."*
- ➢ *"I'm not alone, a lot of people are afraid to drive on the highway."*

New consequences:

- ➢ You feel calmer and more relaxed.
- ➢ You are able to focus on the road.
- ➢ You drive safely and arrive at your destination safely.

In conclusion, the ABC method can help you identify irrational thoughts that contribute to your stress and anxiety. By challenging them and replacing them with more rational and positive thoughts, you can better manage your emotions and behaviors.

Relaxation Skills

Relaxation techniques are effective tools to reduce stress, anxiety and promote a state of calm and relaxation. They are used in a variety of therapeutic approaches, including cognitive-behavioural therapy, to help individuals manage their emotions and physical responses to stress. Here are some of the most commonly used relaxation techniques:

1. **Deep breathing:** Take a few moments to sit comfortably, close your eyes and focus on your breathing. Inhale deeply through the nose, swelling your abdomen, then exhale slowly through the mouth. Repeat this process several times focusing on your breathing, which can help calm the nervous system and reduce feelings of anxiety. Here's how to do it:
   - Find a quiet place where you can sit comfortably.
   - Close your eyes and focus on your breath.
   - Inhale deeply through the nose counting to four, feeling your abdomen swell.
   - Hold your breath briefly for a count of four.
   - Exhale slowly through your mouth for a count of four, feeling your abdomen deflate.
   - Repeat this deep breathing process for a few minutes, focusing on the regular rhythm of your breathing and letting distracting thoughts pass without attaching to it.

2. **Progressive muscle relaxation:** Begin by lying down or sitting comfortably. Stretch the muscles of a part of your body, such as the arms, and then release them completely while focusing on the feelings of relaxation. Then move to another part of the body, such as the legs, and repeat the process until you have relaxed all muscle groups. This technique can help release body tension and promote a feeling of overall relaxation. Here's how to do it:

- Lie down or sit comfortably.
- Start with the muscles in your feet. Tension them by contracting the muscles for a few seconds, then release them completely by feeling the relaxation spread.
- Gradually ascend along your body, contracting and relaxing each muscle group, from the legs to the head.
- Take your time to feel relaxation and relaxation every step of the way.
- Pay attention to the feelings of relaxation and lightness in the muscles as you release them.

3. **Guided visualization:** Picture yourself in a quiet and peaceful place, such as a beach or garden. Visualize the details of this place, colors, sounds and sensations. Mentally immerse yourself in this relaxing environment and let your imagination create a soothing experience. This technique can help divert attention from stress and induce a state of deep relaxation. Here's how to do it:
   - Sit comfortably or lie down in a quiet place.
   - Close your eyes and start imagining a peaceful and relaxing place, like a beach or garden.
   - Visualize the details of this place, colors, shapes, sounds and sensations.
   - Try to fully immerse yourself in this mental experience using all your senses.
   - Stay in this guided viewing state for as long as you want, focusing on the feelings of calm and relaxation

4. **Mindfulness meditation:** Sit comfortably and pay attention to the present moment, without judging the thoughts or sensations that emerge. Let thoughts pass without attaching to them, focusing on your breathing or bodily sensations. Mindfulness meditation can help cultivate a state of calmness and presence, reducing mental ruminations and promoting relaxation. Here's how to do it:
   - Find a comfortable sitting position, your feet flat on the floor, your hands resting in your lap.

- Close your eyes and pay attention to your breathing. Notice the movement of air coming in and out of your body.
- Let thoughts pass without attaching to them, simply observing them without judging them.
- Pay attention to your body sensations, such as sensations of contact with the chair, sensations of tension or relaxation in different parts of the body.
- If your mind is moving away from the present moment, gently bring your attention back to your breathing or bodily sensations.

It should be noted that everyone can have different preferences when it comes to relaxation techniques. It can be helpful to experiment with different methods to find the ones that work best for you. In addition, the regular practice of relaxation techniques is generally recommended to fully benefit from them.

Changing automatic thoughts.

Changing automatic thoughts is like redecorating your mental interior. Imagine your mind as a room where automatic thoughts are the old furniture you no longer like. You have the power to replace them with new furniture that better suits your style and makes you happy.

Pourquoi est-ce important ? Automatic thoughts can be like bulky furniture that clutters your mental space and keeps you from feeling comfortable. By changing them, you create a more pleasant and fulfilling mental environment.

How does it work?

1. **Identify automatic thoughts:** Record thoughts that arise spontaneously. And analyze their impact on your mood and behavior.
2. **Challenging automatic thoughts:** Question the validity of these thoughts. And look for evidence for or against these thoughts.
3. **Replace automatic thoughts:** Develop more positive and realistic alternative thoughts. And visualize yourself acting according to these new thoughts.

For example:

➢ Automatic thinking: "I'm going to fail."
➢ Alternative thinking: "I can learn from my mistakes and improve."

In conclusion, changing automatic thoughts is an effective way to reshape your mind to be more positive and more in tune with your aspirations. This can help you feel better about yourself and approach life with more confidence and serenity.

Here is a practical sheet that you can use to put this into practice:

Useful information

To identify your thought patterns, you can keep a journal in which you write down your daily thoughts, or use a mobile app dedicated to managing stress and anxiety. Pay attention to your thoughts and try to analyze them objectively, without judging yourself. Over time, you will develop a better understanding of your thought patterns and be able to manage them more effectively.

Here are some ways to identify your thought patterns:

1. Observe your thoughts:

> - Take time to pay attention to your thoughts, especially in situations that trigger negative emotions.
> - Write down your automatic thoughts on a notebook or in an app.
> - Identify keywords and recurring themes in your thoughts.

2. Question your thoughts:

> - Ask yourself if your thoughts are based on reality or if they are subjective interpretations.
> - Look for evidence contrary to your automatic thoughts.
> - Consider other perspectives on the situation.

3. Explore the origin of your diagrams:

> - Reflect on your past experiences and how they may have influenced your thought patterns.
> - Identify the attachment figures of your childhood and their impact on your development.
> - Understand how your patterns protect you (even if inappropriately) from difficult emotions.

4. Develop alternative thoughts:

> ➢ Reflect on more rational and positive thoughts about the situations that trigger you.
> ➢ Use cognitive restructuring techniques to challenge your automatic thoughts.
> ➢ Learn to speak kindly to yourself and cultivate self-compassion.

Identifying one's thought patterns is a process that takes time and patience. It may be helpful to be accompanied by a therapist or psychologist.

Focus on the present:

Behavioral and cognitive therapy (CBT) is characterized by its focus on the present, meaning it focuses on current problems and present symptoms rather than focusing exclusively on past events. This approach is based on several psychological principles.

1) **The importance of the here and now:** CBT is based on the principle that psychological problems are often rooted in current thought patterns and behaviors. By focusing on the present, therapists can help individuals identify the specific challenges they face in their daily lives and develop strategies to deal with them.

2) **Reducing rumination and avoidance:** By focusing on the present, CBT seeks to reduce excessive rumination about the past and anticipatory anxiety about the future. Rumination is about getting lost in negative thoughts and rehashing past events, while avoidance is about avoiding situations that cause anxiety. By focusing on the present, CBT encourages individuals to actively engage in the present moment and face current challenges rather than getting caught up in negative thought patterns or avoiding difficult situations.

3) **The use of concrete and pragmatic techniques:** CBT focuses on practical and specific interventions that can be implemented in everyday life. It proposes strategies such as mindfulness, problem-solving, modifying dysfunctional behaviors, etc., to help individuals cope with current

difficulties. These techniques enable individuals to develop coping skills and improve their emotional and behavioral functioning in the present.

Step 1: Identify the present difficulties. Become aware of the specific problems and symptoms you are currently experiencing in your daily life. And identify the thought patterns or behaviors that contribute to these difficulties.

Example: *"I am often overwhelmed by anxiety at work and feel unable to cope with professional demands."*

Step 2: Development of adaptive strategies. Identify CBT techniques that can help you cope with your current challenges. And learn practical skills such as mindfulness, problem solving, or changing problematic behaviors.

Example: *"I will practice mindfulness to stay alert and calm at work. I will also use the problem-solving technique to approach difficult tasks in a structured way."*

Step 3: Practice in the present. Apply the strategies learned in your daily life. And actively engage in the present moment and face difficulties rather than avoid them.

Example: Practice mindfulness at work by focusing on your breathing and observing your thoughts and emotions without judgment. Apply problem solving by identifying concrete steps to manage stressful tasks.

By following these CBT steps, you can focus on current issues and develop practical strategies to address them. By actively engaging in the present, you can improve your emotional well-being and overall functioning in your daily life.

The structured and goal-oriented approach:

The structured, goal-oriented approach is one of the key features of behavioural and cognitive therapy (CBT). This approach is based on several psychological and therapeutic principles.

1) **The need for structure and planning:** CBT recognizes the importance of a clear structure and accurate planning of therapeutic sessions. This helps

establish a consistent therapeutic framework and maximize treatment effectiveness. By having a defined structure, therapists and patients can work in a systematic and organized way towards therapeutic goals.

2) **Setting clear treatment goals:** In CBT, the therapist and patient work together to set specific, measurable goals. These goals are usually related to the patient's current difficulties and targeted problems for treatment. Setting clear goals creates a common focus and therapeutic direction, which fosters patient engagement and motivation.

3) **The development of a concrete treatment plan:** Once the objectives have been defined, CBT involves the development of a concrete treatment plan. This plan may include different techniques and specific interventions tailored to the patient's needs. The treatment plan is usually based on proven protocols and evidence-based interventions, which contributes to the effectiveness of the therapy.

4) **Therapist-patient collaboration:** CBT is based on active collaboration between the therapist and the patient. The therapist guides the therapeutic process, provides information and techniques, and helps the patient achieve their goals. The patient is active in their own healing process, actively participates in the sessions and practices the skills learned between sessions.

Step-by-step fact sheet:

Step 1: Setting treatment goals. Work to identify the specific issues you want to address. And set clear, measurable and achievable goals that will help you solve these problems.

Example: *"My therapeutic goal is to manage my social anxiety and develop communication skills to feel more comfortable during social interactions."*

Step 2: Develop a treatment plan. Develop a concrete treatment plan. And identify specific techniques and interventions that will be used to achieve your goals.

Example: The treatment plan may include graded exposure sessions to social situations, cognitive restructuring strategies to challenge negative thoughts, and assertive communication exercises to develop social skills.

Step 3: Implementation of the treatment plan. Actively work to practice the techniques and interventions of the treatment plan. And follow the specific steps defined in the plan, fully engaging in the exercises and recommended practices.

Example: Participate in gradual exposure sessions with the support of your therapist, practice cognitive restructuring by identifying and challenging negative thoughts during social interactions, and practice assertive communication skills in real-life situations.

How to express your feelings and needs?

Talking about what we care about is a skill that has two essential functions for our happiness. First, it allows us to release the emotions we have stored inside. Second, it allows us to build healthy and authentic relationships with others. So how do you express yourself consciously, honestly and directly?

Deeply hidden feelings.

All the most beautiful things in life - love, joy, passion and dreams - make no sense if we can't share them with anyone. It is not for nothing that when we experience great happiness, the first thing we do is to tell our loved ones about it. In a magical way, it intensifies our joy and makes it even more tangible.

Unfortunately, we are no longer as eager to talk about the emotions that are difficult for us. Everything that could portray us in a bad light, we prefer to hide in the depths of ourselves and leave it there once and for all. Anything that could negatively affect our relationship with another person, we prefer to keep to ourselves. We filter our own feelings, experiences and thoughts, choosing only those that are safe and comfortable for both parties.

Why do we do this?

Because we've been taught to shun difficult emotions and avoid delicate conversations. We were taught that there are "bad" and "good" emotions. How many times did we hear in our childhood "don't cry", "calm down", "be wise"? We quickly learned that we should not accept emotions such as anger, sadness, disappointment, guilt. Therefore, we do not know how to manage them and we do not know how to behave when someone around us manifests them. And since we don't accept difficult emotions, not only do we not want to admit them to ourselves. We also don't want to tell others about it because we're afraid they won't accept how we feel either. This fear often has a very solid basis. I have experienced this myself many times when, by sharing what I think and feel with someone, I am greeted with surprise or criticism rather than understanding.

Everyone has a great need for approval and acceptance. Showing others what we have inside carries the risk of being rejected, which is painful even for the strongest people.

Fear of rejection?

The question is why we assume we will be rejected.

It is never possible to accept a difficult emotion at home but not accept it in others (or vice versa). If an emotion makes us uncomfortable, we tend to deny any manifestation of it, regardless of who expresses it. If, on the other hand, we understand that anger, for example, is a natural reaction to certain circumstances, and that we know how to express that anger consciously and safely - we will perceive the anger of others in exactly the same way.

Therefore, when we notice anger or sadness in our loved ones, we often subconsciously activate our own defense mechanisms.

Through our behavior, we show that we do not accept such emotions and that we prefer that the other person keep them to themselves. We do everything in our power to make the other person immediately stop being angry, or we make them understand that sadness is totally useless in a given situation. In doing so, we ensure that the person closes because they have not had the space to freely express their emotions.

It's hard to admit, but in the past, I myself have often obstructed the emotions of my loved ones. When I didn't understand how one could be sad in a given situation, I made it clear to the other person. I saw myself as a "more conscious person" who knew better what could be a source of sadness and what was not. At the time, I did not yet know that I was encouraging the denial and displacement of the feeling that the person was experiencing at that time.

But to return to the question. Why do we assume that by speaking up we will be rejected?

First of all because, as I have just written, this has often happened. Second, because we project our own reactions onto others. As we deny our own difficult feelings, we expect a similar reaction from others when we consider sharing what is playing out in our own souls. We assume that we can't rely on accepting and understanding the "harder" parts of our personality, so we don't even try to express how we feel. We suffocate inside ourselves what so desperately wants to come out.

Unmet needs

The same goes for our needs and desires. We perceive many of them as "displaced" and we are afraid that if we tell another person about it, they think something is wrong with us.

There is another reason why we do not share with others what we are concerned about. Since we fail to manage our feelings ourselves, we often assume that others also have difficulty doing so. So we're afraid of hurting the other person. We believe that what we say will be difficult for them and that we will cause them grief and suffering.

For example, it can be a relationship in which partners spend a lot of time together. A person may need more space for themselves (going out with friends, walking alone). However, they may not communicate this need to the other person for fear of feeling rejected. In this case, not being able to express their need can lead to a situation where the person seeking more freedom for themselves will deny that need, while feeding growing frustration with their partner. The partner will feel this frustration in different ways (mainly through non-verbal messages), but will have no idea what causes it. This can be a source of many conflicts and misunderstandings.

All this pushes us to lock our feelings, needs and desires in an airtight box somewhere in the farthest recesses of our subconscious and do our best to keep them there. Unfortunately, this has quite negative consequences because:

1. Unexpressed feelings accumulate in our bodies as accumulated energy and are often the source of physical ailments or destructive outbursts of anger.
2. Lack of communication in a relationship will always be the source of countless misunderstandings that lead to conflicts that, without further communication, can lead to the end of the relationship.

Thus, unspoken feelings and needs harm us, as well as our relationships.

Speaking up:

Given the dangerous language, full of judgments, conjectures and misinterpretations, that most of us use, the concerns described above are quite valid. "Traditional" communication actually exposes us to a lack of acceptance from the other party, and increases the risk of hurting the other person with our words.

Sometimes a single word of judgment or misinterpretation is enough to trigger unconscious defense mechanisms in our recipient and turn the dialogue into a useless bouncing bullet and a war to be "right". It is then worth remembering this very true quote:

> *" Le plus grand problème en communication, c'est d'avoir l'illusion qu'elle a eu lieu. "*
>
> George Bernard Shaw

The good news is that we can learn another language that leaves no room for the other person's judgment, but focuses on describing our own feelings and experiences. A language that leaves no room for interpretation and that does not stimulate the defence mechanisms of our interlocutor.

One of these languages is Marshall Rosenberg's method of non-violent communication. It is a set of principles that, by focusing on feelings and needs in dialogue, eliminates the possibility of (often very subtle) psychological abuse in our communication.

A closer look at Rosenberg's work makes it clear that it's not just about changing the way we communicate. This is a different way of looking at emotions and needs, our own as well as those of others.

Before any communication, we focus first on internal communication. We need to understand how we feel ourselves. Accepting our inner experiences and listening to our emotions and needs. Only when we know what we think can we begin to express ourselves properly in front of the other person.

Formulating a message based on the NVC model involves four steps:

1. observations. We start with what we have observed. There is no room for conjecture, interpretation, criticism or judgment - here we share the dry facts we observed (for example, instead of saying "You forgot the dinner we had agreed on again, you don't care about me at all". We say "You didn't come home for the dinner we had agreed upon.").

2. Feelings. In the second step, we talk about the specific feelings that appeared in us in relation to the observations we made earlier (for example, instead of evaluatively saying "You are hopeless, you don't love me!", we can say "I feel disappointed and alone as a result").

3 Needs. Here we describe a need or desire that has not been satisfied and that has caused this feeling (for example: "I need to spend more time with you.").

4. Requests. In the last step, we ask the other person for a specific action that could satisfy our need (for example: "I ask you to come back on time when we have an appointment at a specific time"). Caution should be exercised here about the risk of sufficient assessment. If we said, "I ask you to be more respectful of the promises you have made." we would send an implicit assessment - "you are not keeping the promises you have made."

Putting it all together, such a message could read as follows:

"You didn't come home for the dinner we had planned. It makes me feel disappointed and lonely. I need to spend more time with you. I ask you to come back on time when we have an appointment at a specific time."

And here's another example of a message phrased this way:

"You speak to me in a high voice and use words that make me feel disrespected. I would like to be treated with more respect and kindness. I ask you to keep this in mind in our next conversation."

Why does communication under this model work so well?

Because this form of communication does not stimulate the other person's defense mechanisms, which in a split second can turn the dialogue into a mud battle that prevents us from getting to the heart of the conflict.

Of course, this is just a small sample of what the CNV model can do. Think of it as a small inspiration, not an exhaustive description of the method. I strongly encourage you to read the book "nonviolent communication", in which Marshal Rosenberg describes the "language of love", listing many examples to use in practice.

Communication is a vast and fascinating field. It's not enough to get the message across, and as we strive to express ourselves better, it's also helpful to learn the skills that will support our new way of communicating. These include:

- Separating emotions from facts and interpretations,
- Communicate constructively during a conflict,
- Communicate your needs and make requests,
- Mark your limits and communicate them assertively,
- Note the roles we assume during a contact with another person,
- Entering deeper levels of relationships,
- Give feedback and accept compliments.

What happens when we start expressing our feelings and needs openly and directly?

First of all, we gradually begin to free ourselves from the huge ballast we have carried on our shoulders. Emotions that were previously hidden in the recesses of our subconscious are now slowly "released", while at the same time our inner self is put in order. First, we bring them into our own consciousness, and then, using appropriate language, we communicate them to other people.

In this way, we allow them to understand us. This helps to heal our relationships and bring more empathy and understanding to them. In doing so, we avoid unnecessary conflicts and misunderstandings. We empower others to take care of our needs, and we know how to meet the needs of people who are important and close to us.

The art of expressing yourself freely can be a source of many positive changes in the world of your relationships. Learning a language that is non-violent and non-judgmental is certainly not easy. I keep learning it and feel great satisfaction when my efforts have a positive impact on my relationships.

Exercises and examples.

To practice cognitive techniques, here are some simple exercises and examples you can try:

1. **Automatic thought identification:**

    - **Exercise:** Keep a journal of thoughts. Write down thoughts that arise spontaneously in different situations. Become aware of negative or irrational automatic thoughts that contribute to emotional disorders. By recording these thoughts in a journal, you develop a better understanding of your thought patterns.

    - **Example:** You are late for a meeting and you automatically think *"I am always late, I will fail again"*. By noting this, you identify a negative automatic thought.

2. **Challenging automatic thoughts:**

    - **Exercise:** Ask yourself questions to question the validity of your automatic thoughts. For example, ask yourself if you have concrete evidence to support these thoughts.
    - **Example:** You may ask yourself *"Were there times when I managed to be on time?"*.

3. **Replacement of automatic thoughts:**

    - **Exercise:** Develop more positive and realistic alternative thoughts to replace negative automatic thoughts. And you change your perception of the situation.

➤ **Example:** Replace *"I'm always late"* with *"Sometimes I'm late, but that doesn't mean I'm a failure."*

4. **Positive visualization:**

➤ **Exercise:** Visualize yourself succeeding in a situation that is challenging for you. Imagine yourself acting confidently and effectively. The goal is to reinforce positive thoughts by imagining successful scenarios. By visualizing success, you build confidence in your ability to overcome obstacles.

➤ **Example:** Visualize yourself arriving on time at a meeting, calmly controlling the situation. By visualizing yourself arriving on time at a meeting and calmly managing the situation, you strengthen your self-confidence.

5. **Use of mantras:**

➤ **Exercise:** Choose positive affirmations and repeat them regularly to reinforce your new thoughts. By repeating positive affirmations regularly, you train your mind to embrace these new thoughts as a reality.

➤ **Example:** Repeat *"I am able to overcome obstacles"* several times a day to strengthen your confidence in your abilities.

By practicing these exercises regularly, you can gradually change your automatic thought patterns for more positive and constructive thoughts. This can help you improve your emotional well-being and cope with the challenges of everyday life with more confidence and resilience.

Chapter 3: Behavioural techniques.

In this chapter, we dive into the world of behavioral techniques, practical tools to transform our actions and our actions. As Nassim Nicholas Taleb points out, *"What we call chaos is just a very complex order."* Similarly, our behaviors may seem chaotic, but they often follow predictable patterns. By understanding these patterns and modifying them, we can positively influence our daily lives. Behavioral techniques, such as graded exposures, behavioral activation, and time and responsibility management, are concrete ways to learn and change our actions to improve our emotional well-being. Through exercises and concrete examples, we will explore how these techniques can be put into practice to transform our behaviours and quality of life.

Graduated exposures.

Graduated exposure is a technique used in behavioral therapy to help individuals overcome their fears and phobias. This method is based on the principle of gradual exposure to the source of anxiety, which allows the person to gradually get used to the feared situation and thus reduce their level of fear. Imagine that you are afraid of spiders. At first, the very idea of being near a spider can trigger strong anxiety. With graded exposure, you might start by looking at images of spiders, then gradually approach a spider in a terrarium, and finally be able to hold a spider in your hand without feeling intense fear.

Graduated exposure is based on the principle of habituation, that is, the more you are exposed to a source of anxiety, the more your fear decreases over time. This works in part because your brain learns that the dreaded situation is not as dangerous as it initially thought. For example, if you're afraid to speak in public, you might start by practicing speaking in front of a mirror, then in front of a close friend, then in front of a small group, until you feel comfortable speaking in public. By using graded exposure in a regular and structured way, you can gradually overcome your fears and phobias, which can significantly improve your quality of life and emotional well-being.

Example: Fear of spiders.

Escalation

1) Look at a photo of a spider.

2) Watch a spider video.
3) Being in the same room as a caged spider.
4) Touch a stuffed spider.
5) Hold a spider in his hand.

Progressive exposure:

➢ Start by looking at a spider photo for a few seconds.
➢ Gradually increase the duration of exposure and the difficulty of situations.
➢ Use relaxation techniques to manage your anxiety.

Activation comportementale.

Behavioral activation is a technique of behavioral therapy that aims to help individuals overcome depression by encouraging them to engage in activities that give them pleasure and a sense of accomplishment. This approach is based on the principle that activity can positively influence mood and help break the vicious cycle of inactivity and depression. Imagine feeling depressed and having trouble getting up in the morning. Behavioral activation would encourage you to set simple and achievable goals for yourself, like taking a shower, going out to get some fresh air, or doing an activity you love, even if you don't feel like it. By engaging in these activities, you can begin to feel a renewed sense of energy and interest in life, which can help improve your mood and reduce depressive symptoms.

Imagine you're in a deep, dark hole, and with each passing day, that hole gets deeper and deeper. Behavioral activation involves throwing a rope down that hole to start moving up, engaging in activities that help you break out of isolation and regain a sense of control over your life. By practicing behavioral activation regularly, you can gradually regain a satisfactory level of activity and improve your mood and quality of life

Think of your mind as a wasteland garden.

Depression: It is a thick fog that covers the garden and prevents you from acting and enjoying its colors.

Behavioral activation: It is the sun that dispels the fog and allows you to regain the pleasure of gardening and cultivating your well-being.

How does it work?

1.   Identify Activities   3.

> ➤ List the activities you enjoyed doing before your depression.
> ➤ Choose activities in different areas: (social, professional, physical, leisure, etc.
> ➤ Start with simple, short activities.

Planning and commitment

> ➤ Plan the activities you will do.
> ➤ set yourself realistic goals
> ➤ Commit to completing planned activities.

Positively reinforce

> ➤ Reward yourself every time you complete an activity.
> ➤ Record your progress in a journal.
> ➤ Celebrate your successes, even the smallest ones.

Example of a situation: A person with depression has difficulty getting out of bed and bathing.

Activation comportementale:

> ➤ **Simple activity:** Get up and get dressed.
> ➤ **Schedule:** Get up at 9am and get dressed before 10am.
> ➤ **Commitment:** Commit to doing this activity every day.
> ➤ **Positive reinforcement:** Commend yourself for completing the activity and reward yourself with a nice little thing.

Explanation:

> ➤ **Behavioral activation = Clearing the fog of depression:** By resuming positive activities, you clear your mind and regain the desire to live.

> **Pleasant activities = Sunbeams:** They nourish your soul and allow you to cultivate happiness and joy.
> **Progress = Flowers that bloom:** Every little victory is a flower that blooms in your garden and encourages you to keep going.

In conclusion, behavioral activation is an effective technique to fight depression and regain an active and positive life.

Time management and priorities

Time and responsibility management is an essential skill for leading a balanced and productive life. This technique consists of effectively planning your time and organizing your tasks in such a way as to maximize its effectiveness and reduce the stress related to procrastination and work overload. Imagine you have an important project to complete. Using time and responsibility management, you could start by drawing up a list of tasks to be accomplished, ranking them in order of priority. Then you could allocate some time for each task, making sure to take regular breaks to avoid fatigue and burn-out. Finally, you could regularly evaluate your progress and adjust your plan if necessary. As a conductor conducts an orchestra by synchronizing the different instruments to produce harmonious music, time and responsibility management is about effectively coordinating the different tasks and activities in your life to achieve your goals in an effective and balanced way.

Think of your time as a river.

Your responsibilities: These are the rocks and obstacles that dot the riverbed.

Time and responsibility management: This is the art of navigating the river using your energy and resources optimally to achieve your goals.

Why does it matter?

> **Lack of time and responsibility management:** This can create stress, anxiety and a feeling of overwhelm.

> ➤ **Effective time and responsibility management:** This allows you to feel more in control of your life, accomplish your tasks and achieve your goals.

How does it work?

1. Planning

> ➤ do you have clear and realistic objectives ?
> ➤ Break down your goals into smaller, more manageable tasks.
> ➤ Prioritize your tasks based on their importance and urgency.
> ➤ Plan your day and week with a calendar or task management tool.

2. Organization

> ➤ Create a filing system for your documents and tasks.
> ➤ Set a dedicated and tidy workspace.
> ➤ Learn how to manage distractions and stay focused on your tasks.

SPECIFIC TECHNIQUES:

> ➤ Use the Pomodoro technique which consists of dividing the work into short time intervals called "pomodoros", usually 25 minutes, followed by a short break of 5 minutes.
> ➤ Apply the Eisenhower Matrix to prioritize your tasks. It is a time and priority management tool that ranks tasks according to their urgency and importance.

> - Urgent and important: to be done immediately.
> - Important but not urgent: to plan for later.
> - Urgent but not important: to delegate if possible.
> - Neither urgent nor important: to be eliminated or postponed

> ➤ Say "no" to requests that are not prioritized.

Example situation: You are a student and you have a lot of work to do for your exams.

Time management and priorities

> ➤ **Set clear goals:** Pass your exams.

> **Break down your goals into tasks:** Make review cards, learn courses, practice with blank exams.
> **Prioritize your tasks:** Start with the hardest subjects.
> **Plan your day:** Set work and review ranges.
> **Organize your workspace:** Tidy up your desk and remove distractions.
> **Use specific techniques:** The Pomodoro technique to stay focused.

Explanation:

> **Managing time and responsibilities = Sailing the river:** By using your resources optimally, you can achieve your goals and enjoy the journey.
> **Responsibilities = Rocks and obstacles:** They can slow you down, but they can be bypassed or used as stepping stones.
> **Efficient management = Smooth navigation:** You feel in control and move serenely towards your goals.

In conclusion, time and responsibility management is an essential skill for success in your personal and professional life.

By practicing time and responsibility management, you can improve your productivity, reduce your stress and improve your overall quality of life.

Social skills training

Social skills training is an essential part of CBT to combat stress and anxiety. It provides concrete tools to improve social interactions, manage stressful situations and build self-confidence, contributing to a better quality of life.

+ **<u>Assertiveness skills:</u>**

Being assertive means being able to express your needs, opinions and limits in a clear, respectful and effective way. It also involves recognizing and respecting the needs and rights of others.

Step 1: Identify needs, opinions and limitations

Take time to reflect on your needs, opinions, and limitations regarding a specific situation. For example, you might identify the need to take time for yourself, the opinion that your contribution is important, or the limit of not agreeing to be constantly interrupted in your work.

Step 2: Clarity and specificity

Formulate your needs, opinions and limits in a clear and specific way. Avoid generalities and be specific in your communication. For example, instead of saying "I want more free time," you could say "I need two hours a day to relax and recharge."

Step 3: Mutual Respect

Make sure your communication respects the needs and rights of others. Avoid imposing your needs on others and look for solutions that take into account all the interests involved. For example, if you need time for yourself, come up with a solution that also allows the other person to meet their needs, such as finding a time slot that works for both.

Step 4: Using "I" and assertiveness

Use sentences starting with "I" to express your needs, opinions and limitations. This helps to empower your communication and avoid accusing or criticizing others. For example, say *"I feel the need to share my opinion on this topic"* rather than *"You never listen to me"*.

Step 5: Nonverbal Communication

Make sure your body language and tone of voice reflect your assertiveness. Maintain an upright posture, maintain proper eye contact, and use a calm, confident tone of voice.

Step 6: Training and practice

Assertiveness is a skill that improves with practice. Look for opportunities to practice being assertive in real-life situations. Start with less stressful situations and work your way up to more complex ones as you gain confidence.

For example, let's say you need more time for yourself in the evening after work. Here's how you could apply the steps:

- **Step 1:** Identify your need: You need time to relax and recharge after a day of work.
- **Step 2:** Be clear and specific: Express that you need 30 minutes of quiet time each evening to relax.
- **Step 3:** Mutual respect: Offer a solution that also respects the needs of your partner or family, such as agreeing on a time slot where you can have your time calm without disrupting the activities of others.
- **Step 4:** Use assertiveness: Say "I need 30 minutes of quiet time each night to relax and recharge. Would it be possible to find a time that suits everyone?"
- **Step 5:** Make sure your non-verbal communication is aligned with your message. Maintain eye contact, an open posture and use a confident tone of voice. Step 6: Practice this assertive communication regularly to strengthen your assertiveness skills.

By developing your assertiveness skills, you will be able to communicate your needs, opinions and boundaries in a respectful and effective way, while fostering balanced and satisfying relationships with others.

Critique management

Accept constructive criticism in a non-defensive manner, recognizing learning opportunities and avoiding impulsive or aggressive reactions.

Fact Sheet: Critical Management

Criticism management is a valuable skill for accepting constructive criticism in a non-defensive way and turning that feedback into learning opportunities. Here is a step-by-step guide to developing this skill:

Step 1: Receive criticism without reacting impulsively

When you receive criticism, take a mental break to avoid immediately reacting defensively or aggressively. Breathe deeply and take a moment to think before answering. **For example:** A colleague points out that you could improve your organization during team meetings.

Step 2: Actively listen and stay open

Listen carefully to the criticism without interrupting. Be open to the other person's perspective and be ready to understand their perspective. **For example:** Listen carefully to your colleague's suggestions on how to organize meetings and try to understand why they think improvements could be made.

Step 3: Recognize learning opportunities

See criticism as an opportunity to learn and grow. Recognize that even constructive criticism can help you improve and develop new skills.**For example:** Accept that you could benefit from better meeting organization to increase efficiency and productivity.

Ask questions to clarify

If you need more detail or clarification about the criticism, feel free to ask respectful questions to better understand the other person's expectations and suggestions. **For example:** Ask your colleague what specific aspects of meeting organization they think you could improve.

Step 5: Respond constructively

Once you have taken the time to listen and understand the criticism, respond in a constructive and respectful way. Explain how you plan to use this review to improve yourself. **For example:** Respond to your colleague by saying, "Thank you for your feedback. I will take your suggestions into account and work on a better organization of meetings in the future. I appreciate your input to make our team more efficient."

Step 6: Track and apply changes

Be sure to follow up on how you use criticism to make positive changes. Show that you have learned from criticism by implementing concrete actions. **For example:** In future meetings, apply your colleague's suggestions by taking a more organized approach and encouraging the participation of all team members.

By developing critical management skills, you will be able to accept constructive feedback in a non-defensive way and leverage it to improve yourself. An open and receptive attitude will allow you to turn criticism into learning opportunities and strengthen your professional and personal skills.

Each competency is defined below:

✦ **Developing and maintaining friendships:**

Initiate and maintain friendly relationships, show interest and commitment to others, and maintain regular communication.

Fact Sheet: Developing and Maintaining Friendships

Interpersonal skills are essential for developing and maintaining healthy friendships. Here is a step-by-step guide to developing these skills:

<u>Step 1: Initiate Friendly Relationships</u>

Show interest in others: Ask open-ended questions to learn more about people and their lives. Show genuine interest in what they have to say. Example: When meeting someone for the first time, ask them to tell you about their interests or passions.

<u>Step 2: Establish regular communication</u>

Maintain regular contact: Take the initiative to have regular conversations with your friends. Use various means of communication, such as phone calls, text messages, or face-to-face meetings. Example: Call a friend to check in and chat regularly.

<u>Step 3: Show interest and commitment</u>

Be attentive and receptive: Actively listen and empathize with your friends. Show them that you care about their feelings and experiences. Example: When your friend shares a concern or achievement, show empathy and ask questions to learn more.

<u>Step 4: Share quality moments</u>

Create opportunities to spend time together: Plan enjoyable activities and share quality moments with your friends. Organize joint outings, dinners, or activities that strengthen connections. Example: Invite your friends to a picnic, a movie night, or an outdoor hike.

Step 5: Mutual Support

Offer emotional support: Be there for your friends when they are going through difficult times. Listen without judgment and offer support and guidance as needed. Example: If a friend is going through a stressful time, offer your support by actively listening to them and offering helpful solutions or resources.

Step 6: Maintain Authenticity

Be yourself: Stay authentic in your friendships. Don't be afraid to voice your opinions or be vulnerable with your friends. Example: Share your feelings and personal experiences with your friends honestly and being yourself.

By developing these interpersonal skills, you will be able to develop and maintain healthy friendships. Take the initiative to initiate relationships, maintain regular communication, show interest and commitment to others, share quality moments and offer mutual support. These skills will help you build meaningful connections and strengthen your friendships.

⊹ Establishment of Limits

Know how to define and maintain personal limits and respect the limits of others in interpersonal relationships.

Fact Sheet: Setting Boundaries

Knowing how to set and maintain personal boundaries is essential to building healthy interpersonal relationships. Here is a step-by-step guide to developing this skill:

Step 1: Identify your personal limitations

- Take time to reflect on your personal needs, values and preferences. Identify behaviors, situations, or requests that are uncomfortable for you and that you want to limit. **For example:** You can identify that you need time alone each day to recharge your batteries.

Step 2: Be clear and specific

- Express your boundaries in a clear, specific and respectful way. Use affirmative phrases to communicate what you accept and what you don't accept. **For example:** Say "I'd rather have at least 24 hours' notice before accepting an invitation" rather than "I hate it when people ask me out at the last minute."

Step 3: Communicate your limits assertively

- Use assertive communication to express your limits. Be respectful but firm in your expression and be sure to maintain an open posture and a calm tone of voice. **For example:** When someone asks you to do something that goes beyond your limits, confidently respond, "I understand that you need help, but I'm not able to do it right now."

Step 4: Respect others' boundaries

- Recognizing and respecting others' boundaries is just as important as setting your own. Pay attention to the signals and requests of others, and avoid overstepping their personal boundaries. **For example:** If a friend lets you know that they don't want to discuss a specific topic, respect their request and don't push them to talk about it.

Step 5: Face the challenges

- Be prepared to deal with situations where your boundaries may be challenged or violated. Stay firm in your beliefs and don't give in to social pressure or unreasonable demands. **For example:** If someone tries to convince you to go beyond your limits, remember the importance of taking care of yourself and maintain your position.

Step 6: Practice assertive communication

- Practice regularly communicating your limits assertively. The more you practice it, the more natural and effective it will become in your interpersonal interactions. **For example:** Imagine scenarios where you need to express your limits and practice the corresponding assertive responses.

By developing your boundary-setting skills, you will be able to set and maintain clear personal boundaries, respect the boundaries of others, and cultivate healthy and balanced interpersonal relationships. Assertive communication is the key to building respectful relationships where everyone feels listened to and respected within their personal boundaries.

↓ Co-operative skills:

Work effectively as a team, share responsibilities, resolve conflicts constructively and contribute to a common goal.

Fact Sheet: Cooperative Skills

Co-operative skills are essential for working effectively as a team, sharing responsibilities, resolving conflicts constructively, and contributing to a common goal. Here is a step-by-step guide to developing these skills:

Step 1: Establish clear and common goals

Set clear and shared goals with team members. Make sure everyone understands and is committed to these common goals. **For example:** When working on a team project, define the specific objectives to be achieved and ensure that all team members understand and accept them.

Step 2: Sharing Responsibilities

Distribute responsibilities evenly among team members. Identify each member's strengths and skills to maximize each member's contribution. **For example:** In a project team, assign specific tasks to each member based on their skills and interests. Make sure each member clearly understands their responsibilities.

Step 3: Open and transparent communication

Foster open and transparent communication within the team. Encourage the exchange of ideas, active listening and respect for each other's opinions. **For example:** In team meetings, encourage all members to share their ideas and express their concerns. Foster an environment where everyone feels comfortable communicating freely.

Step 4: Constructive Conflict Resolution

In the event of conflicts, take a constructive resolution approach. Listen to different perspectives, seek mutually acceptable solutions, and prioritize compromise. **For example:** If disagreements arise within the team, organize a discussion to allow each member to express their point of view. Encourage the search for solutions that take into account the interests of all members.

Step 5: Collaboration and mutual support

Foster collaboration and mutual support among team members. Encourage the sharing of knowledge, experiences and ideas to achieve common goals. **For example:** Encourage team members to help each other, share knowledge, and offer support when a member is struggling.

Step 6: Assessment and Continuous Learning

Conduct regular assessments to identify the team's strengths and areas for improvement. Use these assessments to learn and improve collectively. **For example:** After a project has been completed, organize a team meeting to evaluate the process, identify successes and challenges, and draw lessons for future projects.

By developing your cooperative skills, you will be able to work effectively as a team, share responsibilities, resolve conflicts constructively, and contribute to a common goal. Cooperation promotes better productivity, smoother communication, and increased team satisfaction.

Social Stress Management Skills:

- **<u>Social Anxiety Management:</u>**

Develop relaxation, self-soothing and breathing techniques to manage anxiety in social situations.

Fact Sheet: Managing Social Anxiety

Social anxiety management involves the development of relaxation, self-soothing and breathing techniques to cope with anxiety in social situations. Here is a step-by-step guide to developing these skills:

Step 1: Knowledge of social anxiety

Learn to recognize the signs and symptoms of social anxiety. Understand negative thoughts and beliefs that may be contributing to your anxiety. **For example:** Be aware of physical signs such as fast heart rate, clammy hands, or negative self-deprecating thoughts that occur in social situations.

4.2:Relaxation techniques .

Learn relaxation techniques to reduce anxiety. This may include methods such as deep breathing, meditation, yoga, or progressive muscle relaxation. **For example:** Practice deep breathing by inhaling slowly through the nose for 4 seconds, holding the breath for 4 seconds, and then exhaling slowly through the mouth for 4 seconds. Repeat several times to relax.

Step 3: Self-soothing

Develop self-soothing strategies to manage anxiety in social situations. Use positive thoughts, affirmations, and reminders of your own worth and skills. **For example:** When you feel anxious in a social situation, tell yourself positive affirmations such as "I am able to feel comfortable and interact with others" or "I am a kind person and worthy of being appreciated".

Step 4: Gradual Exposure

Practice gradual exposure to social situations that generate anxiety. Start with less stressful situations and slowly progress to more difficult ones. **For example:** Start by exposing yourself to small social interactions, such as saying hello to a neighbor, and then progress to more complex situations, such as attending a group meeting.

Step 5: Social Support

Seek support from caring people around you. Share your feelings and concerns with friends or family members who can give you support and encouragement. **For example:** Talk to a trusted friend about your social anxiety struggles. Ask for their support and consider practicing social situations with them to gain confidence.

Step 6: Practice and Perseverance

Practice social anxiety management techniques regularly and persevere in your efforts to overcome anxiety. Accept that progress can be gradual and that every step forward counts. **For example:** Commit to practicing relaxation and self-soothing techniques every day, and deal with social situations with determination and perseverance.

By developing your social anxiety management skills, you will be able to better cope with social situations, reduce your anxiety, and feel more comfortable interacting with others. Be patient, practice regularly, and feel free to seek additional support if needed, such as cognitive behavioral therapy, to help you on your social anxiety management journey.

+ **Managing social pressure:**

Manage peer pressure, social expectations and evaluation situations to maintain a level of trust and calm in social interactions.

Fact Sheet: Managing Social Pressure

Managing social pressure is about coping with social expectations, peer pressure, and evaluation situations while maintaining a level of trust and calm in social interactions. Here is a step-by-step guide to developing these skills:

Step 1: Social Pressure Awareness

- Be aware of social pressure and expectations that can influence your behavior and emotions. Identify situations or times when you feel the most pressure. **For example:** Identify situations such as public presentations, job interviews, or important social events where you feel high social pressure.

Step 2: Challenge unrealistic expectations

- Challenge unrealistic expectations you may have of yourself or those imposed by others. Recognize that you can't please everyone and that it's normal to have imperfections. **For example:** Instead of striving for perfection, accept that you are doing your best and that error is a normal part of learning and growth.

Step 3: Identify your values and priorities

- Identify your personal values and priorities. Determine what is really important to you in order to make decisions that are right for you rather than conforming to the expectations of others. **For example:** Identify your core values such as honesty, authenticity, or work-life balance, and align your actions accordingly.

Step 4: Boost your self-esteem

- Work on your self-esteem by developing a positive perception of yourself. Celebrate your accomplishments, recognize your strengths, and surround yourself with people who support you. **For example:** Keep a journal where you record your achievements, skills, and positive qualities. Practice self-compassion by treating yourself with kindness and understanding.

Step 5: Develop self-soothing strategies

- Develop self-soothing strategies to deal with social pressure. Use relaxation, deep breathing, or visualization techniques to calm your mind and reduce anxiety. **For example:** Before a stressful situation, take a few moments to breathe deeply and imagine yourself feeling calm, confident and able to cope with the pressure.

Step 6: Set healthy boundaries

- Set clear boundaries and stick to them. Learn to say no when you feel overwhelmed or when the demands of others are at odds with your values or priorities. **For example:** If you feel overwhelmed by excessive demands, learn to say no assertively while explaining your limitations and offering alternatives if possible.

By developing your social pressure management skills, you will be able to maintain a level of confidence and calm in social interactions despite social expectations and peer pressure. Stay true to yourself, respect your boundaries, and use self-soothing strategies to cope with evaluation situations and maintain your emotional well-being.

These social skills can be trained through practical exercises, scenarios, role plays and real-life interactions with others. By practicing these skills, you will be able to improve your social fluency, strengthen your interpersonal relationships, and feel more comfortable in social situations.

1. **Scenario:** Create realistic social scenarios where you can practice different social skills, such as verbal and non-verbal communication, active listening, and conflict resolution. For example, simulate a conversation with a colleague, a confrontation with a friend, or an interaction with a stranger.
2. **Role plays:** Play different roles with a partner, where you practice specific social skills. For example, one may play the role of a disgruntled customer and the other the role of customer service, or one may play the role of a new student in a class and the other the role of a welcoming classmate.
3. **Video analysis:** Watch videos or movies featuring social interactions and then discuss them. Analyze character behaviors, identify social skills used, and discuss what worked well and what could have been improved.
4. **Active Observation:** Practice active observation in real-life social situations. Take note of other people's non-verbal behaviors, facial expressions, posture, and tone of voice. Next, reflect on these observations and what you can learn to improve your own social skills.
5. **Communication exercises:** Practice specific skills such as active listening, open-ended questioning, assertive communication, and conflict resolution. You can do this by attending communication workshops or practicing these skills in daily conversations with friends, family members, or colleagues.
6. **Feedback and self-assessment:** After participating in social interactions, seek feedback from your partners or outside observers. Identify your strengths and areas for improvement, and develop a plan to work on those specific skills.

By practicing these exercises regularly and looking for opportunities to apply your social skills in different contexts, you can strengthen your social fluency and improve your interpersonal relationships over time.

Treatment planning and treatment goals

Treatment planning and goal setting are key components of behavioral and cognitive therapy. These processes help define the direction of treatment, identify priority areas for work, and measure progress. Important steps in treatment planning and setting treatment goals include:

Objective setting

The establishment of clear and specific therapeutic goals is essential to guide therapeutic work. Therapeutic objectives must be formulated in a precise, measurable, achievable, realistic and time-bound (SMART) manner.

SMART is an acronym used to describe the essential characteristics of therapeutic objectives:

- **Specific:** The objective must be clearly defined and precise, focusing on a specific area for improvement.
- **Measurable:** The goal must be measurable in order to assess progress. Objective criteria should be used to assess the achievement of the objective.
- **Achievable:** The goal must be realistic and achievable. It must be aligned with the patient's capabilities and resources.
- **Realistic:** The goal must be achievable given the patient's circumstances and constraints. It must be realistic and in line with the patient's expectations and abilities.
- **Time-bound:** The goal must have a specific time limit in order to be evaluated. A period of time must be established to achieve the goal or to observe the progress made.

In summary, SMART is a structured approach to setting therapeutic goals that are specific, measurable, attainable, realistic, and time-bound. This makes it possible to create objectives that are clear, evaluable and adapted to the patient's situation.

Here is a concrete example to illustrate the establishment of therapeutic objectives:

Situation: A person suffers from intense social anxiety and avoids social situations due to fear of judgment and embarrassment.

Therapeutic goal: Reduce social anxiety and improve participation in social situations.

- ➤ **Specific:** Reduce social anxiety specifically related to group situations and social interactions.
- ➤ **Measurable:** Assess social anxiety using validated rating scales, such as the Social Anxiety Scale (sea).
- ➤ **Achievable:** Develop strategies for progressive exposure to social situations to reduce anxiety in a progressive and achievable way.
- ➤ **Realistic:** Consider the patient's abilities and resources, as well as the context in which they operate.
- ➤ **Time-bound:** Establish a realistic timeframe for observing significant improvements, for example, reducing social anxiety by 50% within three months of starting therapy.

Therapeutic strategies to achieve the goal:

- ➤ **Progressive exposure:** Start with less intimidating social situations and gradually increase the level of difficulty by exposing yourself to increasingly complex group situations.
- ➤ **Anxiety Management Techniques:** Learn relaxation, deep breathing and cognitive restructuring techniques to manage anxiety and associated negative thoughts.
- ➤ **Social skills acquisition:** Develop communication, assertiveness and active listening skills to improve social interactions.
- ➤ **Social support use:** Encourage seeking support from trusted people, such as friends or family members, to strengthen social network and sense of security in social situations.

The establishment of therapeutic objectives makes it possible to orient the therapeutic work in a specific way and to measure the progress made. It is important to regularly re-evaluate the objectives to adjust them according to the changing needs of the patient and the results obtained.

Planning therapy sessions.

Once the objectives have been established, the planning of the therapy sessions intervenes. The therapist and patient determine the frequency and duration of sessions, as well as the specific techniques and interventions that will be used.

The planning of therapy sessions takes into account the needs and preferences of the patient, as well as the nature of the problems to be treated. It may involve a combination of cognitive and behavioral techniques, tailored to specific therapeutic goals.

In the case of self-therapy:

In the case of self-therapy, the planning of therapy sessions is based on the individual himself. It is essential to create a structure and framework to support self-therapy and maximize its benefits. Here are some important things to consider when planning self-therapy sessions:

1) **Frequency of sessions:** Determine how often you want to engage in self-therapy sessions. This may vary depending on your needs and availability. You can opt for regular sessions, for example, You decide to engage in self-therapy sessions once a week, every Sunday afternoon, for a period of 30 minutes. You block this schedule in your schedule to ensure you regularly devote time to your emotional well-being.

2) **Duration of sessions:** Set an appropriate duration for your self-therapy sessions. This may vary depending on your preference and ability to engage in a practice of reflection and introspection For example: You set a duration of 20 minutes for your self-therapy sessions. This allows you to focus fully during this period without feeling overwhelmed by a long session. You choose the evening before going to bed to relax and reflect.

3) **Structure sessions:** Develop a structure for your self-therapy sessions to maximize their effectiveness. This can include things like reflecting on past experiences, identifying negative automatic thoughts, evaluating those

thoughts, and practicing specific techniques, such as cognitive restructuring or relaxation. For example: You structure your self-therapy sessions in three parts:

    a. Reflecting on past experiences and feelings,

    b. Identifying negative automatic thoughts and recording them in your thought log.

    c. Practice cognitive restructuring by replacing negative thoughts with more adaptive thoughts.

4) **Use of tools and resources:** Identify tools and resources that can support you in your self-therapy. This may include books, thought journals, online therapy apps, meditation or relaxation audio recordings, and other resources that can enrich your self-therapy experience.

5) **Monitoring and evaluation:** Set up a monitoring and evaluation process to measure your progress and adjust your self-therapy practice if necessary. This may involve keeping a journal of your sessions, noting changes or challenges, and reflecting on the results to make informed decisions for the future.

Here is a simple and clear example of a CBT-based self-therapy session to treat a stress management problem:

STEP 1: PREPARATION

✓ Find a quiet and comfortable place where you can relax undisturbed.
✓ Allow about 30 minutes for this self-therapy session.
✓ Make sure you have a journal or notebook to take notes on.

Step 2: Relaxation

✓ Start with a relaxation technique to relax. This can be deep breathing, guided meditation, or muscle relaxation exercise.
✓ Take a few minutes to focus and concentrate on your breathing.

Step 1: Identifying the issue

✓ Identify the stress management issue you want to address in this session. For example, it could be your overreaction to stress at work.

Step 4: Exploring Automatic Thoughts

- ✓ Reflect on the automatic thoughts that arise when you are faced with stressful situations at work. Jot these down in your journal.
- ✓ Identify negative or irrational thoughts that contribute to your overreaction to stress. For example, "I have to be perfect or I'm a total failure."

Step 5: Evaluating Automatic Thoughts

- ✓ Realistically assess the automatic thoughts you have identified. Look for evidence for and against these thoughts.
- ✓ Challenge the cognitive distortions or errors of reasoning present in these thoughts. For example, ask yourself if this requirement for perfection is realistic and if it actually contributes to your well-being.

Step 6: Cognitive restructuring

- ✓ Replace negative automatic thoughts with more adaptive and realistic thoughts. For example, replace "I have to be perfect or I'm a total failure" with "I do my best and learn from my mistakes, which is normal and humane."
- ✓ Practice these new thoughts by repeating them out loud or writing them in your journal.

action step

- ✓ Develop a concrete action plan to manage your stress response at work. Identify specific strategies, such as taking regular breaks, practicing relaxation techniques during stressful times, or seeking support from colleagues or a therapist.
- ✓ Set yourself measurable and achievable goals to implement these strategies in your daily life.

Step 8: Conclusion

- ✓ Take a few moments to recap what you learned during this self-therapy session.
- ✓ Write down your final thoughts and what you intend to put into practice from now on.

Keep in mind that this example is general and self-therapy may vary depending on specific issues and individual preferences. It is recommended to consult a mental health professional for additional support and more precise adaptation to your personal situation.

Self-therapy requires personal discipline and a commitment to your emotional and mental well-being. By planning your self-therapy sessions, structuring your practices, and using available resources, you can create an environment that is conducive to your personal development and healing.

Progress Monitoring & Evaluation

Monitoring and evaluating progress is essential to assess the effectiveness of treatment and make necessary adjustments. The therapist and the patient regularly evaluate the progress made in relation to the therapeutic objectives set. Different tools can be used to measure progress, such as questionnaires, self-observations, or interviews. These assessments help identify potential improvements and barriers, and adjust the treatment plan accordingly.

Here is an example of a questionnaire commonly used in cognitive behavioral therapy to assess symptoms of depression: Beck's Depression Inventory (BDI). Each question is accompanied by a brief explanation of its purpose and at the end I will provide an explanation of the meaning of the final score.

Each question in the IDB is associated with a point system:

> - **0 points: No symptoms**
> - **1 point: Mild symptoms**
> - **2 points: Moderate symptoms**
> - **3 points: Severe symptoms**

Questionnaire: Beck Depression Inventory (BDI)

1. **Sadness: How often do you feel sad or depressed?** - This question evaluates the frequency of feelings of sadness or depression.

2. **Pessimism: How often do you think nothing will ever get better?** - This question assesses the level of pessimism and hope for the future.

3. **Feeling devalued: How often do you feel devalued or worthless?** - This question assesses self-esteem and self-deprecation.

4. **Guilt: How often do you feel guilty or responsible for things that are not your fault? -** This question assesses the tendency to feel excessively or inappropriately guilty.

5. **Crying: How often do you cry for no apparent reason? –** This question evaluates the frequency of crying for no apparent reason.

6. **Loss of Satisfaction: How often do you feel dissatisfied or unable to enjoy the things you used to enjoy? -** This question evaluates the loss of pleasure or interest in previously enjoyed activities.

7. **Indecision: How often do you have trouble making decisions? -** This question assesses difficulties in making decisions.

8. **Energy loss: How often do you feel tired or lack energy? -** This question assesses energy levels and general fatigue.

9. **Appetite changes: How often have you noticed changes in your appetite (increase or decrease)? -** This question evaluates changes in appetite, such as weight loss or gain.

10. **Suicidal thoughts: How often have you had thoughts of hurting yourself or wanting to die? -** This question assesses the presence of suicidal ideation.

Interpretation of the results:

- ➢ **0-9 points: No depression**
- ➢ **10-18 points: Mild depression**
- ➢ **19-29 points: Moderate depression**
- ➢ **30-63 points: Severe depression**

The final IDB score is obtained by assigning points to each response, according to a predefined scale. The total score is used to assess the severity of depressive symptoms. For example, a higher score indicates more severe depression, while a lower score indicates less severe depression. This score can be used to track the evolution of symptoms over time and assess the effectiveness of treatment. A decrease in the score would indicate an improvement in depressive symptoms.

Regular monitoring and evaluation helps to ensure that the treatment is effective, to make changes if necessary and to maintain the patient's motivation throughout the therapeutic process.

Exercises and examples:

Here are some exercises and examples to practice behavioral techniques:

1. **Behavioral Activation Exercise:**

   ➢ Set yourself a small daily goal, like taking a 10-minute walk.
   ➢ Example: If you're feeling depressed, decide to go outside and get some fresh air for a few minutes, even if you don't feel like it. How do you feel after this activity?

2. **Time and Responsibility Management Exercise:**

   ➢ Make a list of priority tasks for the day.
   ➢ Example: Rank your tasks in order of importance and plan your day by allocating specific time to each task. Use a stopwatch to help you stay focused and meet deadlines.

3. **Graduated Exposure Exercise:**

   ➢ Identify a situation you fear, such as speaking in public.
   ➢ Example: Start by practicing in front of a mirror, then in front of a close friend, before confronting a real public speaking situation.

By practicing these exercises regularly, you can improve your time management, behavioral activation, and graded exposure skills, which can help reduce your stress levels, improve your mood, and feel more in control of your life.

Part 3: My 12-week CBT program

Introduction and preparation.

You are about to start a 12-week journey that will literally transform your relationship with anxiety and stress. Whatever the form or forms your disorders take (generalized anxiety, phobias, OCD, panic disorders, etc.), this cognitive and behavioral program has been proven to achieve significant remission or even complete recovery in more than 70% of patients according to studies.

Why 12 weeks? Because this is the recommended standard time to observe profound and lasting changes in the psychological mechanisms that sustain your anxiety. We will literally reprogram your dysfunctional thought patterns, automatic stress responses, and avoidance strategies.

Over the course of this journey with weekly monitoring, you will gradually gain more perspective on your symptoms, multiply your coping skills, and adopt new constructive mental and behavioral attitudes. Until you regain self-confidence and can lead the fulfilling life that reaches out to you.

The implementation program will be detailed week by week.

Before you start, make sure the time is right in your personal life to fully engage in this demanding but meaningful process. Equip yourself with a logbook to record your thoughts, emotions, exercises and progress throughout these 12 weeks. This will help you maximize your achievements.

Key:

I want to emphasize that a solid foundation has been laid throughout the previous chapters of this book. The concepts, strategies and techniques that we will explore in the coming weeks have all been thoroughly explained and detailed in the previous pages. Every chapter, section, and exercise has been designed to prepare you for this moment. You've learned to identify negative thought patterns, challenge cognitive distortions, practice mindfulness, plan enjoyable activities, and much more. These tools are the foundations on which your therapeutic journey will be based. As we move forward together through these weeks of intense work and personal exploration, I encourage you to regularly refer to previous chapters to strengthen your understanding and mastery of CBT techniques. Each revision will allow you to consolidate your achievements and better prepare yourself for the challenges ahead.

Remember, your commitment to this process is key to getting the most out of it. Take the time to immerse yourself in each chapter, actively practice the proposed exercises, and integrate these strategies into your daily life. Together, we are on the path to healing and emotional well-being. I am confident that with your dedication and perseverance, you can overcome the challenges of anxiety and stress, and achieve a more balanced and fulfilled life.

With all my support,

Week 1: Introduction.

From the beginning of your 12-week journey, it is essential to establish a reliable inventory of your anxiety disorders. We will therefore start by carrying out a detailed assessment of your symptoms to dispel confusion, target the main issues and allow progress to be monitored. With this in mind, I suggest you fill out standard clinical questionnaires that explore the typical manifestations of anxiety disorders, their intensity and their impact on your daily life. This will shed light on possible diagnoses according to official criteria.

NB: the questionnaires in Chapter 3, section: Inventories and self-evaluation scales.

In addition, I invite you to keep a logbook now. This will be a valuable ally throughout the next 12 weeks. Take the time daily to write down the circumstances of your anxieties, their triggers, sensations, thoughts or associated behaviors. This introspection facilitates awareness and resolution of problematic mental patterns. Based on these analyses, we will then define together your personalized goals for the therapy in concrete and realistic terms. This will allow us to adjust the content of the sessions to your specific needs and assess your progress. Finally, you will also learn some easily applicable breathing and relaxation techniques to relieve somatic manifestations of anxiety when they occur.

Thanks to this preliminary work of observation and definition of intentions, you have the solid foundations to begin serenely your cognitive and behavioral reconstruction!

Week 2: Cognitive Restructuring

This week, we're going to explore the power of cognitive restructuring to change your negative thoughts and reduce your anxiety levels.

1. Identify your negative automatic thoughts: Take a moment to observe your daily thoughts. Do you notice recurring thought patterns that are associated with feelings of anxiety or stress? These automatic thoughts can be negative thoughts about yourself, others, or the world around you. Take note of these thoughts and try to identify them when you meet them.

2. Challenge your cognitive distortions: Once you've identified your negative automatic thoughts, it's time to take a closer look. Ask yourself:
- Is this thinking based on real facts?
- Is there objective evidence to support this thinking?
- ARE THERE ANY OTHER WAYS OF MASKING?
- What impact does this thinking have on your mood and behavior?

By questioning your automatic thoughts, you will begin to discover the cognitive distortions that can amplify your anxiety. Identify the most common distortions, such as over-generalization, all-or-nothing thinking, catastrophizing mindset, etc.

3. Sharpen your interpretations: Now that you've begun to question your automatic thoughts and recognize cognitive distortions, it's time to nuance your interpretations of events. Rather than jumping to hasty conclusions or seeing things in a binary way, try to take a more nuanced perspective.

Ask:
- Are there other possible explanations for this situation?
- What concrete facts do I have, and what interpretations do I draw from them?
- How could I see this differently if I take a more balanced perspective?

By nuancing your interpretations, you can reduce the intensity of your negative thoughts and open yourself to more positive and realistic perspectives.

Continue to practice identifying and challenging your negative automatic thoughts throughout the week. Be patient with yourself, as this process can take time. Remember that you are developing important skills to manage your anxiety and stress more effectively.

Week 3: Cognitive restructuring.

This third week marks a new stage in the restructuring of your thought patterns. After identifying your cognitive distortions and starting to question your automatic interpretations, the goal now is to further objectify them. For this, when an anxiety-provoking thought or pervasive worry comes to your mind, you will train yourself to methodically look for objective evidence that would confirm or deny it. Even if it initially requires some effort, this habit is crucial to short-circuit the vicious circle of counterproductive ruminations.

Write down in your diary the evidence for and against found for each negative thought. Examine them in a detached manner. Very often, you will realize how little real basis there is for your anxieties. You will thus begin to formulate more balanced and realistic alternative interpretations of the situation for yourself. This exercise remains essential in the face of your most tenacious concerns about your health, your relationships or your work. Instead of considering them as proven facts, consider them as mere unverified hypotheses. You will realize that there are many other scenarios that are much less anxiety-inducing than those that your anxious mind imagines.

By practicing regularly, cognitive restructuring quickly becomes second nature that protects you from triggering your fears. Step by step, you regain control over your mental life and find serenity!

Week 4: Graduated exposures 1.

This week we will explore graded exposure techniques, a powerful method for gradually overcoming fears and anxieties.

1. Establish a hierarchy of anxiety-provoking situations: Take time to think about the situations that are causing you anxiety and stress. These can be social situations, specific phobias, performance situations, or even intrusive thoughts. Rank these situations in order of severity, starting with those that cause you the least anxiety and ending with those that seem the most formidable.This hierarchy will serve as a guide for planning your graduated exposure exercises, starting with the least anxiety-inducing situations and gradually progressing to the most anxiety-inducing situations.

2. Expose yourself to the least distressing situation: Choose the first situation in your hierarchy, the one that seems the least distressing to you. Commit to voluntarily exposing yourself to this situation for a specified period of time. For example, if it's about talking to a stranger, you might decide to engage in a brief conversation with a salesperson in a store. During this exposure, try to stay open to feelings of anxiety that may arise. Remember that the goal is not to completely remove anxiety, but rather to learn how to tolerate and manage it effectively.

3. Stay in the situation without using an escape route: Once you have exposed yourself to the situation, commit to staying in the situation without seeking an escape route. Avoid avoidance or safety behaviors that might temporarily decrease your anxiety but later reinforce your fears. Allow yourself the opportunity to fully feel your emotions and find that, even if they are uncomfortable, they are tolerable and temporary. Use breathing or relaxation techniques as needed to help you stay calm and centered.

Repeat this graduated exposure exercise every day of the week, choosing a new situation from your hierarchy each time. Take note of the sensations, thoughts, and emotions you experience during and after each exposure, and observe any changes in your response to anxiety over time.

Remember that regular practice of graded exposure can help gradually reduce your anxiety and help you regain a sense of control over your life. Be patient with yourself and continue to engage in this process with courage and determination.

Week 5: Graduated exposures 2.

This week, we will continue to explore graded exposure techniques by gradually increasing the level of difficulty and strengthening your coping skills.

1. Gradually increase the level of difficulty: Now that you have gained experience with the exposure graduated in the previous week, it is time to gradually increase the level of difficulty of the situations to which you expose yourself. Refer to your hierarchy of anxiety-provoking situations that you established in the previous week and choose a slightly more anxiety-provoking situation than the one you previously faced. Commit to exposing yourself to this new situation for a set period of time, using the same techniques as before to tolerate and manage any anxiety that may arise.

2. Practice acceptance of your physical sensations: During your graded exposure exercises, focus on practicing acceptance of your physical sensations. Be aware of your body's reactions to anxiety, such as accelerated heartbeats, rapid breathing, or muscle tension. Rather than fighting these sensations or considering them dangerous, try to accept them simply as your body's natural responses to stress.

Practice breathing or relaxation techniques to help you maintain your calm and balance during exposure, accepting unpleasant physical sensations without seeking to avoid or suppress them.

3. Strengthen your coping skills: Every time you expose yourself to a new anxiety-provoking situation, you strengthen your ability to adapt and cope with anxiety effectively. Remember that every graded exposure experience is an opportunity for learning and growth, even if it may be uncomfortable in the moment.

After each exposure exercise, take time to reflect on what you have learned and what strategies have been effective in managing your anxiety. Celebrate your successes, even the smallest, and be proud of your courage and determination to face your fears.

Continue to practice graded exposure throughout the week, gradually increasing the level of difficulty of the situations you expose yourself to. Keep in mind that the path to recovery can be gradual, but each step you take brings you one step closer to your goal of overcoming anxiety and stress.

Week 6: Letting go.

After several weeks of active work on your thoughts and behaviors, it's time to give yourself a break through letting go techniques. The motive? Get out of automatic mental agitation to accept your emotions with kindness, and cultivate inner serenity. In this week, we will explore techniques to cultivate letting go and mindfulness, essential skills to effectively manage negative thoughts and difficult emotions.

1. Practice mindfulness: Mindfulness is about being fully present and aware of the present moment, without judgment. This practice can help you cultivate a state of calm and serenity, even in the presence of disruptive thoughts or emotions. Try mindfulness exercises such as body scanning, sitting meditation, or mindful walking. During these exercises, pay attention to your body's physical sensations, your breathing, or environmental stimuli, letting thoughts pass without judging or hanging them. Mindfulness can help you detach from negative thoughts and refocus on the present moment.

2. Relax the impact of your negative thoughts: Realize that negative thoughts do not define your reality and that they are only products of your mind. Learn to step back from these thoughts and observe them objectively, without identifying with them. Remember that thoughts are only mental events and are not necessarily true or meaningful. Practice emotional detachment by taking a broader perspective and relativizing the impact of your negative thoughts on your life. The more you can observe your thoughts from a distance, the more you will be able to reduce their power over you.

3. Accept your emotions without reacting to them: Learn to welcome your emotions, whether positive or negative, without trying to judge or suppress them. Emotions are important signals from your inner experience and repressing them can often aggravate feelings of anxiety and stress.

Practice full acceptance of your emotions by recognizing them, naming them, and allowing them to flow freely through you, without seeking to change or control them.

You may find that simply welcoming your emotions with kindness can make them less overwhelming and easier to manage.

Commit to practicing mindfulness, relativizing the impact of your negative thoughts, and accepting your emotions without reacting throughout the week. These skills can help you develop a healthier relationship with your thoughts and emotions, making it easier for you to navigate life's challenges.

Week 7: Behavioral Activation

This week, we're going to focus on behavioral activation, an approach that aims to help you regain control of your life by engaging in positive and rewarding activities.

1. Plan enjoyable and rewarding activities:

Take the time to make a list of activities that give you pleasure and well-being. These activities can be simple, like taking a walk in nature, reading a book, cooking a meal you love, or spending time with loved ones. The important thing is to choose activities that bring you a feeling of satisfaction and joy. Plan at least one enjoyable activity each day and incorporate it into your schedule. Even if you feel anxious or depressed, try to engage in this activity and notice how it can positively influence your mood and well-being.

2. Fragment tasks that seem difficult to you: When faced with tasks or responsibilities that seem overwhelming or insurmountable, break them down into smaller, more manageable steps. This approach will allow you to focus on one step at a time, making the overall task less daunting. Start by identifying the first step of the task and focus only on it. Once this step is complete, move on to the next one, and so on. By fragmenting tasks, you increase your chances of success and reduce your stress levels.

3. Allow for suitable rest periods: It is essential to allow for moments of rest and relaxation in your busy schedule. Give yourself regular breaks to rest and recharge your batteries, especially after completing difficult or stressful tasks.

Use these moments of rest to practice relaxation techniques, such as deep breathing, meditation, or simply to relax and recharge. Listen to the needs of your body and mind, and give yourself permission to take time for yourself. By planning enjoyable activities, fragmenting tasks and providing adequate rest periods, you can promote a healthy balance between activity and rest in your daily life. These strategies can help you manage your anxiety and stress more effectively, while promoting your overall well-being. Continue to engage in these practices throughout the week and observe the benefits they bring to your life.

Week 8: Balancing responsibilities and relaxation.

This week, we will focus on balancing responsibility and relaxation, adopting strategies to reorganize your priorities and promote a better balance in your daily life.

1. Reorganize your priorities: Take a step back to assess your current responsibilities and commitments. Identify tasks and activities that are critical to your well-being and fulfillment, as well as those that may be less important or require less attention. By reordering your priorities, focus on what is really important to you and what contributes to your quality of life. Rank your tasks in order of importance and devote more time and energy to the activities that bring you the most satisfaction and accomplishment.

2. Delegate certain tasks if possible: Feel free to delegate certain tasks or responsibilities to others if possible. Whether at work, at home or in other areas of your life, it can be beneficial to share the burden with others and free yourself from the burden of responsibility. Identify tasks that others could do as well as you, or better, and delegate them accordingly. This can allow you to focus on the most important aspects of your life and reduce your stress levels related to work overload.

3. Alternate work and leisure periods: Practice alternating between work and relaxation periods to promote a better balance in your daily life. Schedule dedicated periods for work or responsibilities, followed by rest and leisure time where you can relax and recharge your batteries.

When working, focus fully on the task at hand, avoiding distractions and using time management techniques to maximize your efficiency. Then, give yourself regular breaks to relax, take a break, and recharge.

By balancing your responsibilities and relaxation, you can reduce your stress levels and improve your overall well-being. Keep reordering your priorities, delegating tasks as needed, and alternating work and leisure time throughout the week. Observe the positive effects these changes can have on your mental and emotional health, and adjust your schedule accordingly to maintain this balance in the long run.

Week 9: Communication and social relations

This week, we're going to focus on the importance of communication and social relationships in managing anxiety and stress.

1. Assert yourself constructively: Practice assertiveness by expressing your needs, opinions, and boundaries in a clear, direct, and respectful manner. Learn to say "no" when you are overworked or can't take on additional responsibilities, and to express your thoughts and feelings openly and honestly. Be aware of your body language and tone of voice, adopting an open posture and using a calm and assertive tone. Assertiveness can help you set healthy boundaries in your relationships and reduce your stress levels related to social interactions.

2. Cultivate empathy in your relationships: Practice empathy by putting yourself in the shoes of others and trying to understand their feelings and perspectives. Actively listen when others are talking to you, paying attention to their words, body language, and underlying emotions. Pay attention to the needs and concerns of others, and offer support and understanding when appropriate. Cultivating empathy in your relationships can strengthen your connections with others and foster a sense of connection and belonging.

3. Ask for help when you need it: Know when you need help and don't hesitate to ask for support when you need it. Whether it's managing your anxiety, overcoming personal difficulties, or solving relationship problems, it's important to know when to seek help and not be afraid to do so.
Talk to a trusted friend, family member, mental health professional, or anyone else in your support network. Sharing your concerns with others can help you feel less alone and find effective solutions to your problems.

By practicing assertiveness, cultivating empathy in your relationships, and asking for help when needed, you can strengthen your communication and social skills, which can help reduce your anxiety and stress. Continue to practice these skills throughout the week and see improvements in your interactions with others and in your overall well-being.

Week 10: Relapse Prevention

This week, we will focus on relapse prevention by adopting strategies to anticipate risk situations, set realistic goals, and maintain learned CBT techniques.

1. Anticipate risky situations: Take the time to identify situations, environments or triggers that could increase your level of anxiety or stress. Whether it's difficult social situations, interpersonal conflicts, important life transitions, or recurring negative thoughts, be aware of factors that could put you in trouble. By anticipating these risk situations, you can better prepare for them and develop appropriate coping strategies. Pay attention to the warning signs of stress and anxiety, and act quickly to manage them effectively.

2. Set realistic goals: Set realistic and achievable goals for yourself, taking into account your abilities, resources and life context. Whether it's goals related to your work, relationships, mental health, or other areas of your life, make sure they're specific, measurable, achievable, relevant, and time-bound (SMART).
By setting realistic goals, you can strengthen your motivation and commitment to take action to improve your overall well-being. Celebrate your progress and successes, even the smallest ones, and be kind to yourself if you encounter obstacles along the way.

3. Maintain some learned CBT techniques: Continue to practice and maintain the CBT techniques you have learned throughout your self-therapy journey. Whether it's cognitive restructuring, graded exposure, mindfulness, or other strategies, incorporate them into your daily routine to bolster your stress and anxiety management skills.
Remember that relapse prevention is an ongoing process and requires a constant commitment to your mental health and well-being. Be proactive in managing your anxiety and stress, using the tools and techniques you have learned to successfully navigate life's challenges. Continue to engage in this process throughout the week and beyond, doing your best to take care of yourself and maintain your emotional balance.

Week 11: Debrief.

This week is the perfect opportunity to take stock of your progress, adjust your strategies if necessary and celebrate your successes!

1. Measure your progress against your goals: Take a moment to assess your progress from the beginning of your journey. Reflect on your initial goals and how you came closer to achieving them. Use monitoring tools like a logbook, self-assessment questionnaires, or measurement scales to quantify your improvements. Identify where you have made significant progress and where you may still need to work. Be honest with yourself in your assessment, but also thankful for the progress you have made so far.

2. Adjust your strategies as needed: Based on your assessment, identify the strategies that have been most effective for you and those that may require adjustments. If some CBT techniques have worked well for you, continue to practice them regularly. On the other hand, if you have encountered obstacles or difficulties with certain strategies, be open to exploring new approaches or changing your approach.

See additional resources, talk to a mental health professional, or seek input from people around you for advice on how to adjust your strategies. Remember that adaptability is an important skill in managing anxiety and stress, and be prepared to explore new avenues to find what works best for you.

3. Celebrate your achievements! Take the time to celebrate your successes, no matter how small. Recognizing and celebrating your progress is key to boosting your motivation, self-esteem, and commitment to your self-therapy journey. Celebrate every milestone, goal, and moment of victory, no matter how big or small.

Celebrate your successes in a way that feels meaningful to you, whether it's by congratulating yourself internally, sharing your accomplishments with loved ones, offering a special reward, or simply taking the time to savor the feeling of pride and accomplishment. You've worked hard to get to where you are, so don't forget to celebrate your journey and everything you've accomplished so far.

Keep using this week to reflect on your journey, adjust your strategies as needed, and celebrate your successes. You are on track to overcome your anxiety and stress, and every small step you take brings you one step closer to your goal of emotional well-being and inner peace.

Week 12:

Congratulations on reaching the final week of your self-therapy journey to overcome anxiety and stress through cognitive behavioral therapy (CBT). This week marks the conclusion of your journey, but also the beginning of a new phase of your life where you are better equipped to face challenges with confidence and resilience. Here are some things to consider to close your journey in a thoughtful and constructive way:

- **Take stock of what you've learned:** Take time to take stock of everything you've learned and accomplished over the past few weeks. Reflect on the skills you have learned, the strategies that have been most effective for you, and the positive changes you have noticed in your daily life. Identify the progress you've made, whether it's lowering your anxiety levels, improving your social relationships, or better managing your emotions. Be aware of the resources you have developed to deal with difficulties, and be grateful for the lessons you have learned from this journey.

- **Keep practicing the helpful exercises:** Even if your self-therapy journey is coming to an end, it doesn't mean you have to give up the techniques and strategies you've learned. Keep practicing the exercises that have been most helpful to you, whether it's deep breathing, mindfulness meditation, cognitive restructuring, or other stress management techniques. Incorporate these practices into your daily routine, adapting them to your needs and lifestyle. Remember that regular practice is essential to maintain your learning and strengthen your anxiety and stress management skills.

- **Congratulate yourself for your efforts:** Finally, take a moment to congratulate yourself for your efforts and commitment to your mental health and well-being. You've done a great job engaging in this self-therapy journey, exploring new skills, and facing your challenges with courage and determination.

- Acknowledge your successes, no matter how small, and be proud of everything you've accomplished so far. You've invested time and energy in your personal development, and it's worth celebrating.

In conclusion, remember that healing from anxiety and stress is an ongoing and evolving process. Continue to engage in your own growth and seek the support you need to maintain your emotional well-being. You have the tools and resources to overcome the challenges ahead, so move forward with confidence and optimism towards a calmer, happier, and more fulfilled future. You are on the right track, and I wish you every success in your future endeavors.

Summary exercises.

Here is a recap of the 12-week exercises for overcoming anxiety and stress through cognitive behavioral therapy (CBT):

Week 1: Introduction and prerequisites

- Complete questionnaires to understand your symptoms.
- Keep a journal to track your thoughts and emotions.

Week 2: Cognitive Restructuring 1

- Identify your negative automatic thoughts.
- Challenge your cognitive distortions.
- Weaken your interpretations by reviewing the evidence for and against.

Week 3: Cognitive Restructuring 2

- Look for objective evidence for or against your thoughts.
- Formulate more realistic alternative thoughts.
- Practice this restructuring on your concerns.

Week 4: Graduated Exhibitions 1

- Establish a hierarchy of anxiety-provoking situations.
- Expose yourself to the least distressing situation.
- Stay in the situation without using an escape route.

Week 5: Graduated Exhibitions 2

- Gradually increase the level of difficulty of situations.
- Practicing the acceptance of one's physical sensations.
- Enhancing coping skills

Week 6: Letting Go

- ➢ Practice mindfulness (body scanning, meditation, etc.).
- ➢ Relax the impact of your negative thoughts.
- ➢ Accepting emotions without reacting to them.

Week 7: Behavioral Activation

- ➢ Plan enjoyable and rewarding activities.
- ➢ Break down difficult tasks into manageable steps.
- ➢ Provide suitable rest periods.

Week 8: Balancing Responsibility and Relaxation

- ➢ Reorganize your priorities to focus your energy on what's essential.
- ➢ Delegate certain tasks if possible to reduce mental load.
- ➢ Alternate work and leisure periods to maintain a healthy balance.

Week 9: Communication and social relations

- ➢ Assert yourself constructively by expressing your needs and limitations.
- ➢ Cultivate empathy in your relationships by actively listening to others.
- ➢ Seek help when needed for social support.

Week 10: Relapse Prevention

- ➢ Anticipate risk situations and develop adaptation strategies.
- ➢ Set realistic goals to maintain motivation.
- ➢ Maintain some learned CBT techniques to reinforce acquired skills.

Week 11:

- ➢ Measure your progress against your initial goals.
- ➢ Adjust your strategies if necessary based on the results.
- ➢ Celebrate your successes, big and small, to build motivation and self-confidence.

Week 12:

- ➢ Take stock of achievements to become aware of your progress.
- ➢ Continue to practice useful exercises in your daily life.

➢ Congratulate yourself for your efforts and for embarking on this journey to emotional wellbeing.

Tips for maintaining achievements.

To maintain the gains made through your self-therapy journey to overcome anxiety and stress with cognitive behavioral therapy (CBT), here are some tips:

1. **Practice learned techniques regularly:** Incorporate breathing, mindfulness, cognitive restructuring, and graded exposure exercises into your daily routine. The more you practice these techniques, the more they will become habits and help you effectively manage your anxiety and stress.
2. **Stay aware of your thoughts and emotions:** Keep a journal to monitor your thoughts and emotions. Identify negative thought patterns and anxiety triggers so you can proactively address them.
3. **Maintain a healthy life balance:** Make sure you maintain a balance between work, play, sleep, and exercise. A healthy, balanced diet can also help reduce stress and anxiety.
4. **Stay connected with your support network:** Continue to maintain positive and rewarding social relationships. Share your successes and challenges with friends, family members, or a mental health professional if needed.
5. **Be alert for signs of relapse:** Stay alert for warning signs of relapse such as increased anxiety, recurrent negative thoughts, or changes in your mood. If you notice these signs, feel free to ask for help and use learned strategies to deal with them.
6. **Keep Educating Yourself About Stress and Anxiety Management:** Stay informed about new research and recommended practices in stress and anxiety management. Books, podcasts, videos and online resources can be useful tools to deepen your knowledge and build your skills.
7. **Be Kind to Yourself:** Be patient and compassionate with yourself during your learning retention journey. Remember that progress is not always linear and it is normal to experience ups and downs. Be self-compassionate and give yourself permission to take care of yourself.

By following these tips and staying committed to your own wellbeing, you will be able to maintain the gains made through your CBT self-therapy journey and continue to progress towards a more balanced and fulfilling life.

Conclusion.

By completing this book, I sincerely hope I have been able to provide you with the tools and knowledge to overcome the anxiety and stress that can sometimes hinder our emotional and mental well-being. Cognitive behavioral therapy (CBT) is a powerful and proven approach to addressing these challenges, and each chapter has been designed to guide you step-by-step through the core principles and techniques of this method.

Over the weeks, you've explored the inner workings of your own psyche, learned to identify and challenge your negative automatic thoughts, confront your fears through graded exposure, and cultivate a mindfulness mindset to fully experience the present moment.

Your commitment and perseverance throughout this journey is to be commended. You have shown courage in facing your fears and making positive changes in your life. Whether you have felt small victories or big successes, each step you take brings you one step closer to your ultimate goal: a life lived with calm, confidence and balance.

I encourage you to continue to practice the techniques you've learned, stay open to learning and growth, and seek the support you need when challenges arise. You deserve well-being and inner peace, and you have the resources to achieve them.

Remember, this book is simply the beginning of your journey towards a more fulfilled and balanced life. Keep moving forward with courage and determination, knowing that you are capable of overcoming anything that stands in your way.

I wish you all the best on your journey to a life free from anxiety and stress, and thank you for choosing to take this first step towards your emotional well-being.

Bonus: Practical techniques to get rid of stress and anxiety.

Why get rid of stress?

Think of your body like a car. Faced with an imminent danger of death (an accident for example), your car starts at full speed thanks to a massive dose of fuel (adrenaline), forgetting everything else. Only survival counts! But this "run forwards" mode can't last too long. Your car is not designed to drive as much as possible at all times, it would eventually let go of you. And this is not sustainable. Intense stress over a short period of time to survive a life-threatening event is manageable. But chronic stress is devastating in the long run.

All energy is monopolized in anticipation of "danger", to the detriment of other functions such as the immune system. As a result, we get sick more easily in the face of viruses and bacteria. 90% of illnesses are linked to stress!

The worst thing is that today stress is practically no longer vital at all. According to one study, our main sources of anxiety are:

> - Silver (78%)
> - domestic work, household chores;
> - Work (60%)
> - Health (56%)
> - Relationships (56%)
> - Terrorism

As we can see, most of these stresses concern the hassles of modern life, not the dangers of death. Our bodies wear out for nothing! So yes, getting rid of chronic stress is essential if you want to stay healthy and enjoy life without anxiety. It's time to regain control of our stress instead of enduring it for no good reason!

Managing stress

There was a time in my life when stress was my constant companion. He wouldn't let go of me. I was mostly stressed by my contact with others ("what will others think of me?") and by the school ("what if I don't pass this test?"). My head was always filled with dark scenarios, the inner critic panicked, and a terrible feeling of warmth settled in my stomach, which burned with every unpleasant thought.

At that time, I was unfamiliar with psychology, personal development, and methods of working with emotions and beliefs. I had no idea how to handle the stress that was eating at me from the inside out. My path to freeing myself from these destructive states took about 2 years and required me to work on myself quite intensively. However, I think you can manage stress in less time - if you have the knowledge I didn't have, when I tried and failed to manage stress. Looking back, I can identify three key levels where it's worth working on stress:

1. **Environmental level** (environment, people, lifestyle)
2. **The level of your body** (physiology, muscle tension, level of stress hormone excreted)
3. **The mind:** The 3rd level of the mind, which is divided into:
    - **Beliefs** (what you believe and how you think).
    - **Mental habits** (what goes on in your head every day).

It is difficult to know which of these two factors has a greater effect. I think it depends a lot on the person. I intuitively feel that body level has been crucial for me. The regular use of relaxation exercises allowed me to "reprogram" the default muscle tension level and the amount of stress hormone secreted, which allowed me to work very easily on my beliefs and mental habits.

Jacobson's progressive relaxation

Have you ever felt a state of complete and deep relaxation, lightness, bliss? Find out what relaxation is and how you can reach this state in just a few minutes. You will get rid of all the tensions, and the stress will disappear like a handful. Relaxing for a few minutes will make you feel good.

But first, do a little experiment:

Try this simple experiment: sit, lean forward, and contract your body as if you were stressed. Now relax and take a deep breath! Think of something stressful. GEN_LBL_SEND_MESSAGE_TO_FEEDBACK_SELECT_3

Stress has probably decreased, hasn't it? This experiment shows how our bodies can influence our emotions.

Negative thoughts trigger stress. It is a physical reaction where muscles contract and cortisol, the stress hormone, is released. But, as you've experienced, changing your posture and breathing can reduce stress.

Jacobson's relaxation, created in the 1920s, is based on this principle. It teaches you to consciously relax your muscles to soothe your mind. By practicing regularly, you will significantly reduce your stress and you will be calmer and more focused on a daily basis.

"A disturbed mind cannot exist in a relaxed body. »

- Edmund Jacobson

Jacobson's relaxation practice will help you significantly reduce your stress and tension levels throughout the day. Your focus and ability to cope with difficult situations will increase. You will be more relaxed and calmer. If you practice regularly, after about two weeks, these effects will persist not only for some time after exercise, but already throughout the day, every day. The positive effects of this type of relaxation exercise are very clear, so you will notice them quickly.

Objective: Reduce stress and muscle tension, improve relaxation and overall well-being.

Duration: The practice can last from 10 to 30 minutes, depending on your availability and needs.

Materials needed: A quiet place, a carpet or a comfortable chair.

Instructions:

1. **Find a quiet place:** Choose a place where you can be quiet and comfortable.

2. **Adopt a comfortable posture:** Sit or lie down comfortably with your arms along your body.

3. **Gradually release the muscles:** Start with the feet and gradually work your way up to the head, contracting and releasing each muscle group for a few seconds. For example, squeeze your toes, then release. Do the same for the calves, thighs, buttocks, abdomen, arms, shoulders, neck and face.

4. **Breathe deeply:** As you relax the muscles, inhale deeply through your nose as you inflate your belly, then exhale slowly through your mouth.

5. **Visualize relaxation:** While you practice muscle relaxation, visualize a feeling of warmth and relaxation invading every part of your body.

6. **Focus on the sensations:** Focus your attention on the feelings of relaxation and release in your muscles.

7. **Repeat if necessary:** You can repeat the exercise for muscle groups that remain tense.

8. **Finish gently:** Once you have relaxed all the muscles, take a few moments to rest and enjoy the feeling of relaxation.

Frequency: For best results, practice this Jacobson relaxation technique once or twice a day, or whenever you feel tense or stressed.

Note: Consult a healthcare professional if you have any health issues or muscle pain before starting any relaxation program.

The TRE method.

I will introduce you to another method that is as simple but powerful, very effective in the therapeutic field and beyond:trauma releasing exercises (TRE). These exercises help relieve some of the stress and tension we accumulate. Although there is already information on this method on the web, I would like to add some indications that I find relevant.

Let's take the example of the deer, which, in order to survive, flees danger by releasing hormones that allow it to escape. Once he is safe, he starts shaking to release the accumulated stress hormones. A striking example is that of a polar bear under great stress by people wanting to examine it:

- **Video title:** Trauma bear
- **Video link:** https://youtu.be/et4060geodi

It turns out that the human body uses the same mechanism.

History of the TRE method.

The TRE method was discovered by observing the natural response of tremors in the body after a traumatic event. Its creator, David Berceli, a missionary in war zones, made observations on the reactions of the local populations. For example, when he was in a bomb shelter in Beirut in 1979, he noticed that everyone there instinctively curled up when they heard the sirens announcing the arrival of the warplanes. Then, in Sudan, he observed that children shook uncontrollably during the bombings, while adults repressed their tremors so as not to show their distress to the children. These observations prompted him to explore the nature of these tremors, which he identified as vital for physical, emotional, and psychological recovery after trauma.

Years later, after studying bioenergetic analysis, Berceli created the TRE method to help reduce stress caused by trauma. Psychologists have noted that young children naturally shake in stressful situations, but as we grow older, we learn to repress our emotions, thus losing this natural ability.

It is important to understand that tremors are a natural and healthy reaction of the body to release emotional tension, but that society often pushes us to fight them by considering them negative. However, by repressing our emotions, we strengthen our bodies and move away from who we really are. The TRE method aims to regain this natural ability to manage emotions to release accumulated tensions and regain a state of relaxation.

The method:

The "TRE" method is easy to learn: a few simple exercises trigger muscle tremors that start in the legs and can go up the body, passing through the pelvis, hip, abdomen, chest, shoulders and jaw. These tremors release deep, chronic muscle tension from the body's "energy center," including the psoas and paraspinal muscles, by spreading along the spine and outward, relaxing tension from the sacrum to the skull. They often start in the legs and pelvis before moving up the body. TRE is considered an effective method for releasing stress, easy to learn alone or in a group.

My ERT experience:

During my first session of TRE (Tension & Trauma Releasing Exercises), I experienced something really strange. After a short warm-up and the first few exercises, my body started vibrating on its own. These vibrations were not as strong as those that can be felt by typing in the search bar of Youtube "TRE", but they were present. I could stop them by changing position, but in the specific position I had to hold, they occurred naturally, without me provoking them. My task was to find the position that made them stronger and maintain it comfortably.

After about 45 minutes of exercise, I felt a deep sense of well-being. I felt like my whole body was soothed, as if every cell had become silent. My head was calm, present and quiet. These sensations persisted for about 3 hours after the session.

After following a few sessions with a professional, you can continue the exercises at home.

Here's how TO practice ERT:
1. **Positioning:** Sit comfortably in a chair or lie on your back. Make sure you have a private area where you feel safe TO practice ERT.
2. **Focus on tension:** Close your eyes and focus on areas of tension in your body. Identify places where you feel stress or discomfort, such as the neck, shoulders, stomach, or any other part of your body where you feel tension.
3. **Tapping:** Use your fingers or the palm of your hand to gently and regularly tap the areas of tension you have identified. Start by tapping lightly, then

gradually increase the pressure if it feels comfortable. You can alternate between soft and firmer taps to explore what works best for you.
4. **Breathing:** While tapping, also focus on your breathing. Take deep, slow breaths, inhaling through the nose and exhaling through the mouth. Let your breath help you release more of your body's tensions.
5. **Expression of emotions:** As you practice TRE, allow yourself to feel and express any emotions that emerge. Don't judge your feelings, but let them flow freely through your body. You may cry, scream, laugh, or feel any other emotion that arises.
6. **Observations:** After tapping for a few minutes, take a moment to observe the physical and emotional sensations that occur in your body. Notice changes in your stress, anxiety, or tension levels.
7. **Repeat:** Repeat this ERT practice AS often as necessary to relieve stress and anxiety. You can practice daily or as often as you like to maintain your emotional well-being.

The Emotional Release Technique can be a powerful tool for managing stress and anxiety. By incorporating this practice into your daily routine, you can learn to release accumulated tensions in your body and cultivate a greater sense of calm and emotional well-being.

The advantages of "TRE:

There are some studies on the empirical validity of this method and we will mention two of them. One was carried out by Maceda (2013) in Brazil to evaluate the effects of the TRE technique in cases of gender-based violence, the results of which suggest that the application of this technique is effective as a therapeutic tool, since it offers effective strategies to prevent violence and reduce stress levels, traumatic symptoms and dissociative behaviours. The other is a pilot study of workers at Children's Villages in South Africa, the results of which suggest that systematic and repeated activation of the self-induced tremor mechanism offers promising therapeutic value.

Finally, let us recall the advantages of applying the technique as a therapeutic tool, in addition to psychotherapy. In addition to promoting the restoration of body balance, this technique increases the chances of success of verbal therapy. It should also be noted that it is advisable to use the TRE technique in a therapeutic context, as its application could activate the release of emotions and memories associated with trauma. Nevertheless, in the case of personal use of the technique, the experiment will be under the control of the person, who will be able to regulate the intensity of the tremors according to the level he can tolerate. Caution is recommended and it will always be best to practice alone after learning the procedure with the help of a therapist.

Exercises to Stimulate the Vagus Nerve and Reduce Stress

Nerves are peripheral structures of the nervous system that communicate between the body and the brain. They also allow us to move and feel sensations such as pain, heat or tickles. And, among the many nerves that spread from head to toe, one of them certainly stands out: the vagus nerve runs through a large part of our body and is directly related to emotions.

What is the vagus nerve?

The vagus nerve, or pneumogastric nerve, is a crucial part of our nervous system, which connects the brain to many vital organs such as the heart, lungs, stomach, and intestines. Its name, "wave", evokes its dispersion through the body, as it ramifies widely to touch many organs. Imagine it as a communication highway between the brain and internal organs, transmitting signals in both directions. For example, when you're stressed, the vagus nerve transmits signals from the brain to the heart to speed up the heartbeat. Conversely, vagus nerve stimulation can lead to a decrease in heart rate and a feeling of calm.

Physiologically, the vagus nerve plays an essential role in regulating many of the body's automatic functions, such as breathing, digestion, and heart rate control. It is also involved in the stress response, influencing the release of hormones like cortisol. It is also linked to our mental well-being. Studies have shown that adequate vagus nerve stimulation can help reduce anxiety and depression. This can be done through simple techniques like deep breathing and activation of the parasympathetic system.

In summary, the vagus nerve is a key player in our nervous system, playing a crucial role in many vital functions. Its stimulation can have beneficial effects on our mental and physical health, promoting relaxation and regulating the automatic functions of the body.

YOU ARE WHAT YOU EAT

You are what you eat, the saying goes, and science has been confirming this for centuries: a balanced diet is essential to staying healthy. But how do the foods we eat actually affect our bodies, and how is the vagus nerve involved in all of this? To understand, we must first talk about the microbiome.

The microbiome is like a miniature city populated by microorganisms that live in different parts of our body, especially our intestines. These tiny inhabitants play a key role in our health by protecting us from harmful invaders and helping us digest food. But for these beneficial foods to reach our brains, they have to take a special path, and that's where the vagus nerve comes in.

This nerve, which connects our gut to our brain, is essential in the communication between these two organs. As neuroscientist John Cryan of University College Cork in Ireland explains, "what happens in the vagus nerve can even affect our emotions." In other words, what we eat can have a direct impact on our mental well-being. Certain foods are particularly beneficial to our microbiome. Plain yogurts, kefir and kombucha, for example, are rich in good bacteria that help balance our intestines. Fruits, vegetables and green vegetables, on the other hand, are rich in fiber, which nourishes the microorganisms in our bodies. By stimulating our microbiome with these foods, we can positively influence our vagus nerve, which in turn sends signals to our brain to regulate our emotions. This gut-brain connection has opened up new perspectives in the field of health, with the use of probiotics and prebiotics to balance our microbiome and improve our mental well-being.

In sum, diet plays a crucial role in our mental and physical health by influencing our microbiome and **activating the vagus nerve**. So, the next time you choose what to put on your plate, remember that you are feeding not only your body, but also your mind.

How to stimulate the vagus nerve?Haut du formulaire

There are several ways to stimulate the vagus nerve, an important part of our nervous system. Stimulation can be useful for a variety of reasons, including to treat medical conditions like tachycardia or depression, or simply to promote relaxation and well-being.

Vagus nerve stimulation can be done in different ways. Some are more formal, such as diagnostic or therapeutic stimulation performed by health professionals. Others are more informal, such as practicing deep breathing, meditation, or even massage. Stimulation methods include carotid sinus massage, Valsalva maneuver, cold water immersion, deep breathing, and swallowing. These methods can help activate the vagus nerve and induce a state of calm and tranquility.

Some ways to stimulate the vagus nerve are:

There are several ways to stimulate the vagus nerve, and it is necessary to know the correct indications and techniques to achieve them.

1. Polyvagal Exercise: This exercise aims to stimulate the vagus nerve and eliminate anxiety, worries and fears. Lie on your back on a carpet or, standing, lean against a wall. Cross your fingers (as if you were going to snap them together) and place your hands behind your head. Your shoulder will lean against the floor or wall. Without turning your head, look as far to the left as you can for 60 seconds. Then look to the right, also for 60 seconds. Repeat the movements, until you sigh, yawn or feel the release of tension.

Sighing or yawning is a sign that the vagus nerve has been activated and is sending positive energy into the body. In fact, any stretching exercise that relieves tension in the neck and shoulders while looking left and right will activate the vagus nerve.

There are videos on YouTube that teach this exercise, sometimes with slight variations. To search in English, type "polyvagal exercises". Opening these videos usually puts your patience to the test because the presenter wants to give a speech. One of these videos can be seen on the website: https://www.youtube.com/watch?v=gHBpHl0oebo.

2. Massage: You can stimulate the vagus nerve with a good physiotherapist specialized in this field. The specialist performs a series of massages in the abdominal area. This vagus nerve stimulation relieves intestinal spasms and activates the parasympathetic nervous system.

3. Diaphragmatic breathing: As mentioned above, the abdominal trunk of the vagus nerve is responsible for the parasympathetic nervous system. This is why breathing in the abdominal tract is soothing.

Lie on your back, put your hands on your stomach. Inhale through your nose, blowing air into your abdomen (you will feel your arms rising). Exhale with your mouth. Try to do this exercise slowly enough to hold only 10 cycles of inspiration-expiration in 2 minutes. This exercise can also be done in a sitting position. It is useful to imagine that you have a red balloon in your belly that you pump with your own breath, or a leaf that goes up or down in your belly. Thanks to this technique, practiced daily, the feeling of stress and anxiety decreases, the heart rate calms down, internal balance and digestion improve.

4. Abdominal muscles: Another effective method of stimulation is to contract the abdominal muscles as if you are about to receive a blow there. Tense muscles allow good stimulation of the vagus nerve. (Saldmann, 2017) It is interesting to test the tension by giving yourself a very slight punch in the abdomen. Once you have tested your resistance in this way, repeat the exercise (already without the punches) fourteen times, alternately contracting and releasing the abdominal muscles.

5. . Exercice en position debout. This exercise is used in dietetics to suppress hunger attacks. Do this before a meal, in a sitting position. Fill your mouth with warm water so that your tongue is submerged and your cheeks are swollen. Do not open your mouth or change your voltage for 3 minutes. At least that is the model portrayed in the media.

After this time, the liquid may be swallowed or spat out. The feeling of hunger is replaced by a feeling of satiety thanks to the signal that the vagus nerve thus stimulated sends to the brain.

6. Strengthening the signal: There are also other ways to stimulate the vagus nerve to strengthen its signal. These means are the vagal maneuvers are measures likely to normalize the heartbeat. They stimulate the vagus nerve which belongs to the autonomic nervous system and participates in the regulation of the heart rhythm. Many cardiac patients learn from their doctor how to use these maneuvers to end their rhythm disorders themselves.

Fact Sheets - Vagus Nerve Stimulation Techniques

1. Carotid massage: Place two fingers on the side of your neck, just under your jaw. Massage gently in circular motions for 30 seconds on each side. Do not massage too hard and stop if you feel pain.

2. Pressure on closed eyes: its purpose is to increase intraocular pressure and stimulate the vagus nerve. You need to close your eyes and place your thumbs on your eyelids, just above the eyeballs. Apply gentle pressure for 10 seconds. But don't massage too hard and stop if you feel pain.

3. Abdominal pressure: You should lie on your back and place your hands on your stomach. Exhale completely and then, holding your breath, contract your abdominal muscles as if trying to lift your belly off the floor. Hold pressure for 30 seconds then release. Repeat 5 times. Do not practice this technique if you are pregnant or have abdominal problems.

4. Drink a cold drink: Its purpose is to stimulate the vagus nerve by causing a cold reaction in the pharynx. To achieve this, you must quickly drink a cold drink, ideally carbonated. (Avoid drinks that are too sweet or acidic.)

5. Increase saliva production: Its purpose is to stimulate the vagus nerve by increasing saliva production. And for that you have to chew a sugar-free gum or suck a hard candy.

6. Inner ear massage: Take a cotton swab and gently massage the inside of your ear for 30 seconds. Do not insert the cotton swab too deep into the ear.

7. Throat rinsing: Take a sip of cold water and gargle for 30 seconds. Avoid this technique if you have throat problems.

8. Diaphragmatic singing: Place one hand on your belly and inhale deeply using your diaphragm (your belly should lift). Exhale slowly as you sing a low tone. Practice and rehearse several times.

9. Trendelenburg Position: Its purpose is to increase venous return and stimulate the vagus nerve. And to achieve this you need to lie on your back and elevate your legs about 30 cm from the ground. Hold for Do not practice this technique if you have heart or circulatory problems.

10. Cold and alternating showers: The purpose of this technique is to stimulate the vagus nerve by alternating hot and cold. You need to start with a hot shower for 2 minutes, then finish with a cold shower for 30 seconds. Repeat the alternation 3 times. You should always start and end with a hot shower.

11. Sleep on your left side: Lie on your left side with your legs slightly bent. If you have breathing problems, consult your doctor before practicing this technique.

13. In case of extreme urgency: Chew sugar-free gum in case of anxiety or panic attack.

Remember that these techniques are not a substitute for medical treatment. If you suffer from anxiety, depression or other disorders, it is important to consult a mental health professional.

Caution: Do not exaggerate the stimulation.

The vagus nerve is an important nerve that plays a role in many vital functions, including digestion, breathing, blood circulation, and heart function. Stimulating the vagus nerve can be beneficial for mental and physical health, but it is important not to exaggerate.

Here are some reasons why vagus nerve stimulation should not be exaggerated:

- **Side effects:** Excessive vagus nerve stimulation can cause unpleasant side effects, such as nausea, vomiting, dizziness, bradycardia (slowed heart rate), and syncope (fainting).
- **Decreased efficiency:** If the vagus nerve is over-stimulated, it may become less sensitive to stimulation, which may reduce the effectiveness of stimulation techniques.
- **Health risks:** In some cases, excessive stimulation of the vagus nerve can be dangerous, especially for people who have heart or circulatory problems.

Here are some tips to avoid over-stimulating the vagus nerve:

- Start with short, gentle stimuli.
- Gradually increase the duration and intensity of stimulation.
- Listen to your body and stop if you experience any unpleasant side effects.

In conclusion, vagus nerve stimulation can be an effective technique for improving mental and physical health, but it is important not to exaggerate. Follow the recommendations of health professionals and listen to your body to avoid unpleasant side effects.

Overcoming stress with EFT:

Emotional Freedom Techniques (EFT) is an alternative psychotherapy method that combines traditional Chinese medicine (TCM) techniques with principles of modern psychology. It is often used to reduce stress and anxiety, as well as to treat emotional trauma. EFT is based on the principle that negative emotions are caused by disturbances in the body's energy system. By tapping on certain acupuncture points while focusing on a specific emotional problem, one purports to release these disturbances and restore energetic balance, which can lead to a reduction in emotional symptoms.

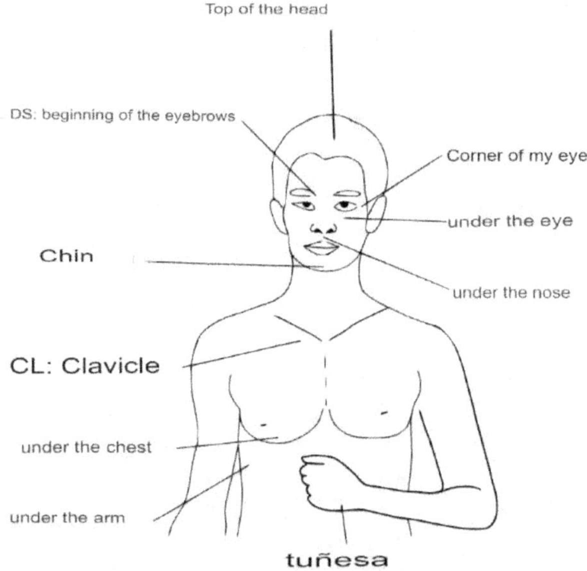

The basic technique of EFT is to focus on a specific emotional problem while tapping lightly with the tips of our fingers, on acupuncture points located on the face and upper body. These points include the top of the head, the corner of the eye, under the eye, under the nose, under the mouth, on the collarbone and under the arm. When tapping on these points, you need to focus on the emotional problem you want to solve. For example, if you're stressed about a particular situation, you might focus on that situation while tapping on acupuncture points.

Although EFT is often touted as an effective method for reducing stress and anxiety, there is little scientific evidence to support its effectiveness. Some studies have suggested that it may be useful in reducing symptoms of stress and anxiety, but more research is needed to confirm these findings.

In conclusion, EFT is an alternative method that may be useful for some people with stress and anxiety. However, it is important to consult a qualified health professional before trying this technique, especially if you have underlying mental or physical health issues.

Here's how EFT can help you beat stress:

> - **Understanding your emotions:** EFT allows you to identify and understand the emotions that are causing you stress.
> - **Changing your negative thoughts:** By focusing on positive affirmations during point stimulation, you can replace negative thoughts that contribute to stress.
> - **Reduce physiological stress activation:** Stimulating acupuncture points sends signals to the brain that can help calm the nervous system and reduce muscle tension.

EFT Fact Sheet for Removing Stress and Anxiety

1. Choose a stressful situation or emotion.
2. Rate the intensity of your stress on a scale of 0 to 10 (0 being no intensity and 10 the maximum intensity).
3. Formulate a positive affirmation sentence that includes your name and acceptance of the emotion. **For example:** "Even though I feel this stress (name the emotion), I accept myself and choose to feel better."
4. Identify acupuncture points to stimulate (look at the previous image).
5. Gently tap the acupuncture points while repeating the positive affirmation at the same time as tapping.

Start with the eyebrow and finish with the wrist. You can tap each point 3-5 times.

6. Repeat steps 4 and 5 until the intensity of your stress decreases.

Tips:

> You can use a diagram or video (youtube) to help you identify acupuncture points.
> If you have difficulty focusing on the positive affirmation, you can simply repeat the name of the emotion.
> EFT can be practiced alone or with the help of a therapist.

EFT is a simple and effective technique that you can use to overcome stress and anxiety. By practicing EFT regularly, you can improve your emotional and physical well-being.

Remember that EFT is not a substitute for medical or psychological follow-up if your stress is chronic or intense.

Conclusion:

Ideally, when people realize something is wrong, they should take steps to avoid situations that make them uncomfortable. Unfortunately, it is not always possible to control the origin of suffering. Almost always, people consult a specialist when the snowball has already become a disease and, even so, ***many prefer to take medication and continue at the same pace, instead of eliminating the source of the problem, which requires more work.***

Learning to manage stress requires, first of all, a life assessment. Often, sources of annoyance can be managed: leaving early to avoid traffic jams and fear of being late, talking to a colleague who doesn't respond when you greet them, etc. Reason and self-knowledge can show you that you need to say "no" more often or look for a more rewarding job, for example. But there are problems that don't just depend on the person.

When to Seek Help

It is often necessary to rely on help to learn how to manage stress. When the situation already involves symptoms of anxiety or depression, or when the problem appears to be rooted in personality, a psychologist or psychiatrist may be helpful. Changing your lifestyle is also fundamental to avoiding the negative consequences of stress. The following is suggested:

➢ **Forest Bathing:** The practice is also indicated as therapy in Japan, where it has even gained its own term. "Forest bathing," or shinrin-yoku , emerged in the 1980s as a form of psychological and physical therapy. The "bath" consists of spending time in the forest to soak up its atmosphere in order to reach a certain state of well-being and reconnect with the green spaces of the country. Several studies have examined the benefits of Japanese practice. Scientists have found that "forest bathing" has a significant impact on your immune system, increasing by 50% the so-called "natural killer cells," a type of lymphocyte necessary for the innate immune system to function.

- ➢ **Going out to fight stress:** In the long run, nature can significantly reduce the level of human stress. Studies have shown that exposure to green spaces can have a significant impact on cortisol levels in saliva, which is a marker of stress. Even the singing of birds or the sounds of a forest can bring us benefits. Others have shown that exposure to green spaces is associated with reductions in blood pressure and heart rate, which have a significant impact on heart disease risk. And it's not just the green landscapes that have a profound impact on our bodies and brains - it seems that even the sounds of nature can really change our brain activity. Whenever you hear the soft sounds of birdsong or a stream, brain MRIs show that your attention naturally turns outward, you are less involved in your own thoughts - and it helps reduce your stress and anxiety levels.
- ➢ **Good sleep:** Chronic lack of sleep has been shown to increase cortisol levels. It's no wonder that without good sleep, people become more responsive, irritated, and eat more. Having a well-defined routine, relaxing in the evening with baths and self-massages, as well as turning off electronic devices at least an hour before falling asleep are tips to avoid insomnia.
- ➢ **Exercise regularly:** Exercise stimulates the production of endorphins that promote well-being, sleep and relaxation, and therefore provides a shield against the effects of stress. In addition, movement helps channel anger and frustration, which is therapeutic. A simple walk can bring relief in tense moments. Finally, engaging in an activity or sport improves self-esteem and a sense of self-care, which also makes a difference in the face of adversity.
- ➢ **Eat a balanced diet:** Many people eat in a hurry and spend many hours on an empty stomach, and the symptoms of hypoglycemia can be mistaken for those of anxiety. Stimulants such as caffeine and excess sugar can also be detrimental to well-being.
- ➢ **Observe your addictions:** It is common to use alcohol or drugs as a form of self-medication during times of overload, which will only create new problems. If you feel like you're doing too much, ask for help.
- ➢ **Having support:** It's important to have someone you trust, whether it's a friend, relative, spiritual counselor, or therapist. According to studies, just knowing you can talk to someone helps you, even if you don't ask them for help.

- ➤ **Practice abdominal breathing:** diaphragmatic breathing is natural for babies, but over the years, you start to breathe only with the thorax, which is not always enough to oxygenate the brain. This basic attitude is the starting point for almost all relaxation techniques because it really works.
- ➤ **Incorporate fun into your routine**: lunch with friends, watching good movies, walking in the park, making love, cuddling a pet, practicing a hobby... everyone has their own way of cultivating well-being. These activities must be present during difficult times. If you have lost the ability to feel pleasure, seek help from a psychologist or psychiatrist.
- ➤ **Meditate:** Several studies prove the effects of different meditation techniques on stress management. One of the benefits of these practices is learning to deal with one's own thoughts and sensations with detachment, which increases self-control.
- ➤ **Seek help:** Relaxation techniques, biofeedback, neurobiofeedback, acupuncture, dancing, self-help groups, as well as cultivating a philosophy of life are all measures that can improve your relationship with stressful stimuli.

Merci pour votre lecture et bonne chance